Collecting and Representing Data

How Many Pockets?
How Many Teeth?

Grade 2

Also appropriate for Grade 3

Karen Economopoulos
Tracey Wright

Developed at TERC, Cambridge, Massachusetts

Dale Seymour Publications®

The *Investigations* curriculum was developed at TERC (formerly Technical Education Research Centers) in collaboration with Kent State University and the State University of New York at Buffalo. The work was supported in part by National Science Foundation Grant No. ESI-9050210. TERC is a nonprofit company working to improve mathematics and science education. TERC is located at 2067 Massachusetts Avenue, Cambridge, MA 02140.

**This project was supported, in part,
by the**
National Science Foundation
Opinions expressed are those of the authors
and not necessarily those of the Foundation

This book is published by Dale Seymour Publications®, an imprint of the Alternative Publishing Group of Addison-Wesley Publishing Company.

Editorial Management and Production: McClanahan & Company
Managing Editor: Catherine Anderson
Project Editor: Alison Abrohms
Series Editor: Beverly Cory
ESL Consultant: Nancy Sokol Green
Production/Manufacturing Director: Janet Yearian
Production/Manufacturing Coordinator: Shannon Miller
Design Manager: Jeff Kelly
Design: Don Taka
Illustrations: Meryl Treatner
Cover: Bay Graphics

 Printed on Recycled Paper

**DALE
SEYMOUR
PUBLICATIONS®**
P.O. BOX 10888
PALO ALTO, CA 94303

Order number DS21651
ISBN 1-57232-220-9
1 2 3 4 5 6 7 8 9 10-ML-00-99 98 97 96

TERC

INVESTIGATIONS IN NUMBER, DATA, AND SPACE

Principal Investigator Susan Jo Russell

Co-Principal Investigator Cornelia C. Tierney

Director of Research and Evaluation Jan Mokros

Director of K–2 Curriculum Karen Economopoulos

Curriculum Development

Joan Akers
Michael T. Battista
Mary Berle-Carman
Douglas H. Clements
Karen Economopoulos
Anne Goodrow
Marlene Kliman
Jerrie Moffett
Megan Murray
Ricardo Nemirovsky
Andee Rubin
Susan Jo Russell
Cornelia C. Tierney
Tracey Wright

Evaluation and Assessment

Mary Berle-Carman
Jan Mokros
Andee Rubin

Teacher Support

Anne Goodrow
Liana Laughlin
Jerrie Moffett
Megan Murray
Tracey Wright

Technology Development

Michael T. Battista
Douglas H. Clements
Julie Sarama

Video Production

David A. Smith
Judy Storeygard

Administration and Production

Irene Baker
Amy Catlin
Amy Taber

Cooperating Classrooms for This Unit

Rose Christiansen
Brookline Public Schools, Brookline, MA

Lisa Seyferth
Carol Walker
Newton Public Schools, Newton, MA

Consultants and Advisors

Deborah Lowenberg Ball
Marilyn Burns
Ann Grady
James J. Kaput
Mary M. Lindquist
John Olive
Leslie P. Steffe
Grayson Wheatley

Graduate Assistants

Kent State University:
Kathryn Battista, Caroline Borrow, Judy Norris

State University of New York at Buffalo:
Julie Sarama, Sudha Swaminathan,
Elaine Vukelic

CONTENTS

Teacher Notes

Investigations in Number, Data, and Space is a K–5 mathematics curriculum with four major goals:

- to offer students meaningful mathematical problems
- to emphasize depth in mathematical thinking rather than superficial exposure to a series of fragmented topics
- to communicate mathematics content and pedagogy to teachers
- to substantially expand the pool of mathematically literate students

The *Investigations* curriculum embodies an approach radically different from the traditional textbook-based curriculum. At each grade level, it consists of a set of separate units, each offering 2–6 weeks of work. These units of study are presented through investigations that involve students in the exploration of major mathematical ideas.

Approaching the mathematics content through investigations helps students develop flexibility and confidence in approaching problems, fluency in using mathematical skills and tools to solve problems, and proficiency in evaluating their solutions. Students also build a repertoire of ways to communicate about their mathematical thinking, while their enjoyment and appreciation of mathematics grow.

The investigations are carefully designed to invite all students into mathematics—girls and boys; diverse cultural, ethnic, and language groups; and students with different strengths and interests. Problem contexts often call on students to share experiences from their family, culture, or community. The curriculum eliminates barriers—such as work in isolation from peers, or emphasis on speed and memorization—that exclude some students from participating successfully in mathematics. The following aspects of the curriculum ensure that all students are included in significant mathematics learning.

- Students spend time exploring problems in depth.
- They find more than one solution to many of the problems they work on.
- They invent their own strategies and approaches, rather than relying on memorized procedures.
- They choose from a variety of concrete materials and appropriate technology, including calculators, as a natural part of their everyday mathematical work.
- They express their mathematical thinking through drawing, writing, and talking.
- They work in a variety of groupings—as a whole class, individually, in pairs, and in small groups.
- They move around the classroom as they explore the mathematics in their environment and talk with their peers.

While reading and other language activities are typically given a great deal of time and emphasis in elementary classrooms, mathematics often does not get the time it needs. If students are to experience mathematics in depth, they must have enough time to become engaged in real mathematical problems. We believe that a minimum of 5 hours of mathematics classroom time a week—about an hour a day—is critical at the elementary level. The plan and pacing of the *Investigations* curriculum are based on that belief.

For further information about the pedagogy and principles that underlie these investigations, see the Teacher Notes throughout the units and the following books:

- *Implementing the* Investigations in Number, Data, and Space® *Curriculum*
- *Beyond Arithmetic: Changing Mathematics in the Elementary Classroom*

The *Investigations* curriculum is presented through a series of teacher books, one for each unit of study. These books not only provide a complete mathematics curriculum for your students, they also offer materials to support your own professional development. You, the teacher, are the person who will make this curriculum come alive in the classroom; the book for each unit is your main support system.

While reproducible resources for students are provided, the curriculum does not include student books. Students work actively with objects and experiences in their own environment and with a variety of manipulative materials and technology, rather than with workbooks and worksheets filled with problems. We also use the overhead projector as a way to present problems, to focus group discussion, and to help students share ideas and strategies. If an overhead projector is available, try it as suggested in the investigations.

Ultimately, every teacher will use these investigations in ways that make sense for his or her particular style, the particular group of students, and the constraints and supports of a particular school environment. We have tried to provide with each unit the best information and guidance for a wide variety of situations, drawn from our collaborations with many teachers and students over many years. Our goal in this book is to help you, as a professional educator, implement this mathematics curriculum in a way that will give all your students access to mathematical power.

Investigation Format

The opening two pages of each investigation help you get ready for the student work that follows. Here you will read:

What Happens—a synopsis of each session or block of sessions.

Mathematical Emphasis—the most important ideas and processes students will encounter in this investigation.

What to Plan Ahead of Time—materials to gather, student sheets to duplicate, transparencies to make, and anything else you need to do before starting.

Exploring Numerical Data

What Happens

Session 1: Quick Data Collections The class works together to create different types of graphs in response to numerical data questions posed by the teacher.

Sessions 2 and 3: Pocket Towers Students answer survey questions for use in Sessions 4 and 5. Then they collect data by building towers that represent the number of pockets they are wearing. Together they discuss ways to organize these pocket towers. Each pair of students organizes a class set of pocket towers to create their own representation of the class pocket data. They draw a picture of their representation.

Sessions 4 and 5: Class Surveys Pairs of students choose one of the survey questions that they answered in Session 2 to investigate further. Students organize and represent a class set of survey data from one question. They share their representations in groups, then discuss systems for keeping track with the whole class.

Mathematical Emphasis

- Collecting data
- Keeping track of data
- Organizing numerical data
- Creating representations
- Seeing representations as a way of communicating to others
- Describing and interpreting representations

Art 7-1-IDF

What to Plan Ahead of Time

Materials

- Inch graph paper (Session 1)
- Student math folders: 1 per student (Session 1)
- Chart paper (Sessions 1–3)
- Scissors, markers, tape (Sessions 1–5)
- Large paper: 2–3 per student (Sessions 2–5)
- Interlocking cubes: class set (Sessions 2–5)
- Color tiles or other manipulatives: class sets (Sessions 4 and 5)
- Class list of names: 2–3 per student (Sessions 2–5)
- Plastic bags or shoe boxes: 1 per group (Sessions 2 and 3)

Other Preparation

For Session 1
- Duplicate Student Sheet 1, Weekly Log, 1 per student. At this time, you may wish to duplicate a supply to last for the entire unit and distribute the sheets as needed. Prepare a math folder for each student if you haven't done so previously.
- Prepare the Number of Letters in Our Name graph by taping two pieces of chart paper together horizontally. You will need to create a range from 0 to 10 (or more) depending on the names in your class. The numbers on the graph will not be evenly spaced. Since the length of the graph paper strips that students will be posting will vary, the placement of numbers on the graph should reflect this. Cut strips of graph paper 1 box

to 10 boxes and use these as a guide for measuring how much space to leave.
- Cut inch graph paper into strips. To determine the length of each strip, allow one box per letter and make all strips as long as the longest name in the class. If a name like Stephanie is the longest name, prepare a 1"-by-9" strip for each student.

For Sessions 2 and 3
- Duplicate Student Sheet 2, Surveys, 1 per pair. Cut apart the student sheets, providing 1 survey form to each student.
- Prepare a class list of names and duplicate 1 per student.
- Prepare a class list of names on chart paper. The order of the names should match those on the student list.
- If you have previously have used an *Investigations* unit and have gathered Pocket Data, display it again for discussion during this session.
- Duplicate the Family letter (p. 100), 1 per family. Remember to sign and date the letter before copying.

For Sessions 4 and 5
- Duplicate the class list of names, 1 per pair.
- Gather students' completed Student Sheets 2, and duplicate 1 class set per pair.

Sessions Within an investigation, the activities are organized by class session, a session being a one-hour math class. Sessions are numbered consecutively throughout an investigation. Often several sessions are grouped together, presenting a block of activities with a single major focus.

When you find a block of sessions presented together—for example, Sessions 1, 2, and 3—read through the entire block first to understand the overall flow and sequence of the activities. Make some preliminary decisions about how you will divide the activities into three sessions for your class, based on what you know about your students. You may need to modify your initial plans as you progress through the activities, and you may want to make notes in the margins of the pages as reminders for the next time you use the unit.

Be sure to read the Session Follow-Up section at the end of the session block to see what homework assignments and extensions are suggested as you make your initial plans.

While you may be used to a curriculum that tells you exactly what each class session should cover, we have found that the teacher is in a better position to make these decisions. Each unit is flexible and may be handled somewhat differently by every teacher. While we provide guidance for how many sessions a particular group of activities is likely to need, we want you to be active in determining an appropriate pace and the best transition points for your class.

Start-Up The Start-Up section at the beginning of each session offers suggestions for how to acknowledge and integrate homework from the previous session and which Classroom Routine activities to include sometime during the school day.

Classroom Routines Routines provide students with regular practice in important mathematical skills such as solving number combinations, collecting and organizing data, and understanding time. There are three classroom routines that occur regularly throughout the grade 2 *Investigations* curriculum, and a fourth one that occurs in the Geometry and Fractions unit, *Shapes, Halves, and Symmetry.*

Session 3

Comparing Lost Teeth Among Other Grades

What Happens

Students post the teeth data that they collected as homework. As a class they make and discuss predictions about collecting teeth data from other classes. In pairs they write and draw plans and organize materials so that they can collect data the following day. Their work focuses on:

- making predictions about data based on a small sample
- planning and organizing a data collection project

Start-Up

Today's Number

Calendar Date *and* Number of School Days Suggest that students use doubles as you work together brainstorming ways to express Today's Number. For example, if students are working on the number 28, some possible expressions are: 14 + 14; 7 + 7 + 7; and 10 + 10 + 4 + 4. If students are working with a larger number, such as 149, some possible expressions are: 50 + 50 + 20 + 20 + 4 + 4 + 1 and 75 + 75 − 1. Add a card to the class counting line and also fill in another number on the blank 200 chart if you are keeping track of the number of days in school.

How Many Teeth Do You Have? Ask students to share their methods from the homework for how they counted their teeth. If you plan to use these data, arrange for a place where students can post them.

Materials

- Prepared grade-level posters (6 sheets)
- Prepared index cards (about 20)
- Class list of names from other classrooms
- Materials for data collection
- Student Sheet 4 (1 per student)

Activity

As students arrive in the classroom, they write their homework data on the prepared grade-level posters. One way to organize the data is to list two columns on each poster labeled *Name* and *Number of Teeth Lost.*

For the last two math classes we have been organizing data about the number of teeth lost by students in our classroom. Yesterday we discussed how our teeth data might compare to a set of data from another second grade class.

Review the list of ideas from yesterday's discussion.

Looking at Sibling Teeth Data

Session 3: Comparing Lost Teeth Among Other Grades ■ 55

One of two classroom routines, Today's Number or How Many Pockets?, is integrated into the Start-Up of most sessions. The third routine, Time and Time Again, appears as a Start-Up in the final unit, *Timelines and Rhythm Patterns,* but is not integrated directly into other units. Instead it is offered as a resource of activities about understanding time and the passage of time. This routine can be integrated throughout the school day and into other parts of the classroom curriculum.

Classroom routines offer students opportunities to build on a familiar activity by integrating experiences from previously taught units. For example, in the routine Today's Number, students write number sentences to equal the number of days they have been in school. Variations of this routine include using addition and subtraction to express the number, using multiples of 5 and 10 to express the number, and using more than three addends.

Most classroom routine activities are short and can be done whenever you have a spare 10 minutes—

maybe before lunch or recess or at the beginning or end of the day. Complete descriptions of each classroom routine can be found at the end of each unit.

Activities   The activities include pair and small-group work, individual tasks, and whole-class discussions. Students are seated together, talking and sharing ideas, during all work times. Students most often work cooperatively, although each student may record work individually.

Choice Time   In most units, there are sessions that are structured with activity choices. In these cases, students may work simultaneously on different activities focused on the same mathematical ideas. Students choose which activities they want to do and cycle through them.

You will need to decide how to set up and introduce these activities and how to let students make their choices. Some teachers set up choices as stations around the room while others post the list of available choices and have students collect their own materials and choose their own work space. You may need to experiment with a few different structures before finding a setup that works best for you, your students, and your classroom.

Tips for the Linguistically Diverse Classroom   At strategic points in each unit, you will find concrete suggestions for simple modifications of the teaching strategies to encourage the participation of all students. Many of these tips offer alternative ways to elicit critical thinking from students at varying levels of English proficiency, as well as from other students who find it difficult to verbalize their thinking.

The tips are supported by suggestions for specific vocabulary work to help ensure that all students can participate fully in the investigations. The Preview for the Linguistically Diverse Classroom (p. 14) lists important words that are assumed as part of the working vocabulary of the unit. Second-language learners will need to become familiar with these words in order to understand the problems and activities they will be doing. These terms can be incorporated into students' second-language work before or during the unit. Activities that can be used to present the words are found in the

appendix, Vocabulary Support for Second-Language Learners (p. 97).

In addition, ideas for making connections to students' language and cultures, included on the Preview page, help the class explore the unit's concepts from a multicultural perspective.

Session Follow-Up

Homework   Homework is not given daily for its own sake but periodically as it makes sense to have follow-up work at home. Homework may be used for (1) review and practice of work done in class; (2) preparation for activities coming up—for example, collecting data for a class project; or (3) involving and informing family members.

Some units in the *Investigations* curriculum have more homework than others, simply because it makes sense for the mathematics that's going on. Other units rely on manipulatives that most students won't have at home, making homework difficult. In any case, homework should always be directly connected to the investigations in the unit or to work in previous units—never sheets of problems just to keep students busy.

Extensions   These follow-up activities are opportunities for some or all students to explore a topic in greater depth or in a different context. They are not designed for "fast" students; mathematics is a multifaceted discipline, and different students will want to go farther in different investigations. Look for and encourage the sparks of interest and enthusiasm you see in your students, and use the extensions to help them pursue these interests.

Family Letter   A letter that you can send home to students' families is included with the blackline masters for each unit. We want families to be informed about the mathematics work in your classroom; they should be encouraged to participate in and support their children's work. A reminder to send home the letter appears in one of the early investigations. These letters are also available separately in Spanish, Vietnamese, Cantonese, Hmong, and Cambodian.

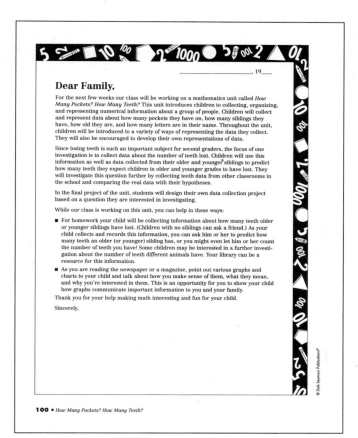

How you incorporate the computer activities into your curriculum depends on the number of computers you have available. Suggestions are offered in each unit for how to organize different types of computer environments.

Children's Literature

Every unit in the grade 2 *Investigations* curriculum offers a suggested bibliography of children's literature that can be used to support the mathematical ideas presented in the unit. This bibliography is found on the Materials List located in the front of each unit.

Some of the grade 2 units have class sessions that are based on a selected children's book. Although the session can be taught without the book, using it offers a rich introduction to the activity.

Literature selected for the units and the bibliographies is limited to books that can offer students strong connections to the mathematics they will investigate.

Technology

Calculators and computers are important components of the *Investigations* curriculum.

Calculators are introduced to students in the second unit, *Coins, Coupons, and Combinations*, of the grade 2 sequence. It is assumed that calculators are a readily available material throughout the curriculum.

The grade 2 *Investigations* curriculum uses two software programs that were developed especially for the curriculum. *Shapes* is introduced in the Introductory unit, *Mathematical Thinking at Grade 2,* and used again during the Geometry and Fractions unit, *Shapes, Halves, and Symmetry.* *Geo-Logo* is introduced and used in the Measurement unit, *How Long? How Far?* Although the software is included in only these three units, we recommend that students use it throughout the year. As students use the software over time, they continue to develop skills presented in the units.

Materials

A complete list of the materials needed for the unit is found on p. 12. Some of these materials are available in a kit for the grade 2 *Investigations* curriculum. Individual items can also be purchased as needed from school supply stores and dealers.

In an active mathematics classroom, certain basic materials should be available at all times: interlocking cubes, pencils, unlined paper, graph paper, calculators, and things to count with. Some activities in this curriculum require scissors and glue sticks or tape. Stick-on notes and large chart paper are also useful materials throughout.

So that students can independently get what they need at any time, they should know where these materials are kept, how they are stored, and how they are to be returned to the storage area. Many teachers have found that stopping 5 minutes before the end of each session so that students can finish what they are working on and clean up is helpful in maintaining classroom materials. You'll find that establishing such routines at the beginning of the year is well worth the time and effort.

Student Sheets

Reproducible pages to help you teach the unit are found at the end of this book. These include student recording sheets as well as masters that can be used as teaching tools.

Many of the field-test teachers requested more sheets to help students record their work, and we have tried to be responsive to this need. At the same time, we think it's important that students find their own ways of organizing and recording their work. They need to learn how to explain their thinking with both drawings and written words, and how to organize their results so someone else can understand them.

To ensure that students get a chance to learn how to represent and organize their own work, we deliberately do not provide student sheets for every activity. We recommend that your students keep a math folder so that their work, whether on reproducible sheets or their own paper, is always available to them for reference.

Name _____ Date _____

Student Sheet 4

Planning a Data Collection Project

1. What are you collecting data about? _____

_____

2. Whom will you collect data from? _____

3. What question will you ask? _____

_____

4. How will you collect these data? What's your plan? _____

_____

_____

_____

5. What materials will you need? _____

_____

_____

_____

_____

_____

104 ■ *How Many Pockets? How Many Teeth?*

Help for You, the Teacher

Because we believe strongly that a new curriculum must help teachers think in new ways about mathematics and about their students' mathematical thinking processes, we have included a great deal of material to help you learn more about both.

About the Mathematics in This Unit   This introductory section (p. 13) summarizes the critical information about the mathematics you will be teaching. This will be particularly valuable to teachers who are accustomed to a traditional textbook-based curriculum.

Teacher Notes   These reference notes provide practical information about the mathematics you are teaching and about our experience with how students learn. Many of the notes were written in response to actual questions from teachers, or to discuss important things we saw happening in the field-test classrooms. Some teachers like to read them all before starting the unit, then review them as they come up in particular investigations.

Dialogue Boxes   Sample dialogues throughout the unit demonstrate how students typically express their mathematical ideas, what issues and confusions arise in their thinking, and how some teachers have guided class discussions.

These dialogues are based on the extensive classroom testing of this curriculum; many are word-for-word transcriptions of recorded class discussions. The value of these dialogues is that they offer good clues to how students may develop and express their approaches and strategies, helping you prepare for your own class discussions.

Where to Start   You may not have time to read everything the first time you use this unit. As a first-time user, you will likely focus on understanding the activities and working them out with your students. Read completely through each investigation before starting to present it.

When you next teach this same unit, you can begin to read more of the background. Each time you present this unit, you will learn more about how students understand the mathematical ideas. The first-time user of *How Many Pockets? How Many Teeth?* should read the following:

- About the Mathematics in This Unit (p. 13)
- What Is a Representation? (p. 31)
- Dealing with Sensitive Issues: But I Haven't Lost a Tooth Yet (p. 52)
- Different Representations of the Same Data (p. 53)

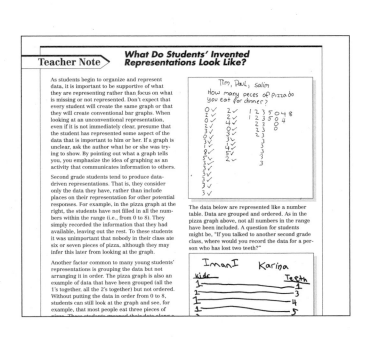

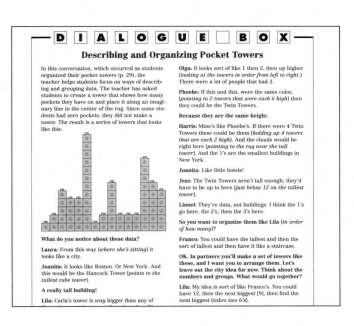

Observing the Students

Throughout the *Investigations* curriculum there are numerous opportunities to observe students as they work. Teacher observations are an important part of ongoing assessment. Individual observations provide snapshots of a student's experience with a single activity. A series of observations over time can provide an informative and detailed picture of a student that is useful in documenting and assessing his or her growth. They are important sources of information when preparing for family conferences or writing student reports.

For many activities, we offer observation guidelines and suggestions. These include what to look for as students work, or questions you might ask to give you insight into their thinking or to stimulate further exploration of an activity.

Teacher Checkpoints The Teacher Checkpoints provide a time for you to pause and reflect on your teaching plan, observe students at work, and get an overall sense of how your class is doing in the unit. These sections offer tips on what you should be looking for and how you might adjust your pacing. Are most students fluent with strategies for solving a particular kind of problem? Are they just starting to formulate good strategies? Or are they still struggling with how to start?

Depending on what you see as students work, you may want to spend more time on similar problems, change some of the problems to use smaller numbers, move quickly to more challenging material, modify subsequent activities for some students, work on particular ideas with a small group, or pair students who have good strategies with those who are having more difficulty.

In *How Many Pockets? How Many Teeth?* you will find these Teacher Checkpoints:

> Creating a Representation (p. 36)
> Organizing and Representing Teeth Data
> (p. 61)

Embedded Assessment Activities Use the built-in assessments included in this unit to help you examine the work of individual students, figure out what it means, and provide feedback. From the students' point of view, the activities you will be using for assessment are no different from any others; they don't look or feel like traditional tests.

These activities sometimes involve writing and reflecting, a brief interaction between student and teacher, or the creation and explanation of a product.

In *How Many Pockets? How Many Teeth?* you will find this assessment activity :

> Looking at Representations (p. 86)

Teachers find that the hardest part of the assessment is interpreting students' work. If you have used a process approach to teaching writing, you will find our mathematics approach familiar. To help with interpretation, we provide guidelines and questions to ask about students' work. In many cases, a Teacher Note with specific examples of student work and a commentary on what they indicate is included. This framework can help you determine how your students are progressing.

As you evaluate students' work, it's important to remember that you're looking for much more than the "right answer." You'll want to know what their strategies are for solving the problem, how well these strategies work, whether they can keep track of and logically organize an approach to the problem, and how they make use of representations and tools to solve the problem.

Ongoing Assessment Good assessment of student work involves a combination of approaches. Some of the things you might do on an ongoing basis include the following:

- **Observation** Circulate around the room to observe students as they work. Watch for the development of their mathematical strategies and listen to their discussions of mathematical ideas.

- **Portfolios** Ask students to document their work in journals, notebooks, or portfolios. Periodically review this work to see how their mathematical thinking and writing are changing. Some teachers have students keep a notebook or folder for each unit, while others prefer one mathematics notebook or a portfolio of selected work for the entire year. Take time at the end of each unit for students to choose work for their portfolios. You might also have them write about what they've learned in the unit.

How Many Pockets?
How Many Teeth?

Content of This Unit   *How Many Pockets? How Many Teeth?* introduces students to organizing and representing numerical data. Students use a variety of materials to collect, organize, and represent the data they gather in ways that make sense to them. Students also explore each other's data representations and some conventional representations such as line plots and bar graphs.

In the first investigation, students keep track of and organize data about the number of pockets worn by students in the class. In another investigation, students collect data about the number of teeth lost by the students in their class. They extend this investigation by collecting data and comparing the numbers of teeth lost by older and younger students. The final investigation involves students in all aspects of data collection and analysis as they design and carry out their own data project.

Connections with Other Units   If you are doing the full-year *Investigations* curriculum in the suggested sequence for grade 2, this is the seventh of eight units. The work in this unit is an extension of the data activities introduced in *Mathematical Thinking at Grade 2* and complements the work with categorical data in *Does It Walk, Crawl, or Swim?*

This unit can also be successfully used at grade 3, depending on the previous experience and needs of your students.

Investigations Curriculum ■ Suggested Grade 2 Sequence

Mathematical Thinking at Grade 2 (Introduction)
Coins, Coupons, and Combinations (The Number System)
Does It Walk, Crawl, or Swim? (Sorting and Classifying Data)
Shapes, Halves, and Symmetry (Geometry and Fractions)
Putting Together and Taking Apart (Addition and Subtraction)
How Long? How Far? (Measurement)
▶ *How Many Pockets? How Many Teeth?* (Collecting and Representing Data)
Timelines and Rhythm Patterns (Representing Time)

Investigation 1 • Exploring Numerical Data

Class Sessions	Activities	Pacing
Session 1 (page 18) QUICK DATA COLLECTIONS	How Old Are the Kids in Our Class? How Many Siblings Do We Have? How Many Letters in Our Names? Introducing Math Folders and Weekly Logs	1 hr
Sessions 2 and 3 (page 26) POCKET TOWERS	Surveys Introducing Pocket Towers Creating a Pocket Representation ■ Homework ■ Extension	2 hrs
Sessions 4 and 5 (page 36) CLASS SURVEYS	■ Teacher Checkpoint: Creating a Representation Class Discussion: Different Ways to Represent the Data ■ Extension	2 hrs

Investigation 2 • Teeth Data

Class Sessions	Activities	Pacing
Sessions 1 and 2 (page 44) HOW MANY TEETH HAVE YOU LOST?	Teeth Towers Making a Line Plot Making a Representation Does the Representation Tell a Story? Class Discussion: Different Ways to Represent the Same Data ■ Homework ■ Extension	2 hrs
Session 3 (page 55) COMPARING LOST TEETH AMONG OTHER GRADES	Looking at Sibling Teeth Data Organizing the Teeth Data Project	1 hr
Sessions 4 and 5 (page 60) COLLECTING TEETH DATA	Collecting Teeth Data from Other Classrooms ■ Teacher Checkpoint: Organizing and Representing Teeth Data Class Discussion: Comparing the Data ■ Extensions	2 hrs
Session 6 (page 67) MYSTERY TEETH DATA	Mystery Teeth Data Which Class Is It? ■ Extension	1 hr

Investigation 3 • Data Projects

Class Sessions	Activities	Pacing
Session 1 (page 76) CHOOSING A QUESTION TO INVESTIGATE	Brainstorming Interesting Questions Planning a Data Project	1 hr
Sessions 2, 3, and 4 (page 81) COLLECTING, ORGANIZING, AND REPRESENTING DATA	Collecting the Data The Data Workshop Interpreting Our Data	3 hrs
Session 5 (page 85) DATA PROJECTS: WHAT DOES THIS GRAPH TELL US?	Making Data Presentations ■ Assessment: Looking at Representations Choosing Student Work to Save	1 hr

Following are the basic materials needed for the activities in this unit. The suggested quantities are ideal; however, in some instances you can work with smaller quantities by running several activities, requiring different materials, simultaneously.

Items marked with an asterisk are provided with the *Investigations* Materials Kit for grade 2.

* Interlocking cubes: about 1000
* Color tiles: class set
* Assorted counters: class sets
  Chart paper
  18"-by-24" construction paper: 1 per pair
* Inch graph paper cut into 1"-by-10" strips: 1 strip per student
  Blank paper or newsprint, 18"-by-24": 2–3 per student
  Large paper, 11"-by-14" or larger: 1 per pair
  Stick-on notes: 1–2 per student plus extras
  Class lists of names: 2–3 per student
  "Master list" of names (class list or list of names on a piece of chart paper or the chalkboard)
  Index cards: about 20
  Clipboards: 1 per pair
  Scissors, markers, tape
  Plastic bags or shoe boxes: 1 per group
  Student math folders: 1 per student
  How Many Teeth? by Paul Showers (optional)

The following materials are provided at the end of this unit as blackline masters.

Family letter (p. 100)

Student Sheets 1–10 (pp. 101–111)

Suggested Bibliography of Children's Literature

Bogart, Jo Ellen. *10 For Dinner.* New York: Scholastic, 1989.

Giganti, Paul Jr. *How Many Snails?* New York: Greenwillow Books, 1988.

Kuskin, Karla. *The Philharmonic Gets Dressed.* New York: HarperCollins, 1992.

Pittman, Helena Clare. *Counting Jenny.* Minneapolis: Carolrhoda Books, 1994.

Showers, Paul. *How Many Teeth?* New York: HarperCollins, 1991.

This unit introduces students to collecting, organizing, and representing numerical data. Most often numerical data are collected through measurement (time, distance, weight) or through counting. This unit engages students in collecting numerical data that can be counted. Questions such as, How many siblings do you have? How many pockets are you wearing? and How many teeth have you lost? are the basis for some of the sorts of information that students will count. In the real world a great deal of numerical information is gathered about groups of people or things. This information is then organized and analyzed and used as the basis for better understanding the group that was studied.

This unit engages students in these critical components of working with numerical data:

Developing Ways to Count and Keep Track of the Data Central to any data collection activity is creating a logical way to count and to keep track of all the data one is collecting or needs to collect. Knowing whom you have counted and whom you still need to count is basic to any data collection activity. Throughout the unit, students discuss various ways of counting and keeping track of the data.

Representing the Same Set of Data in More Than One Way Organizing the same data in more than one way can often make certain features of the data more visible or prominent. Students are introduced to some conventional forms of graphs (bar graph, line plot), and they are also encouraged to create their own ways of organizing and representing data. Our world is flooded with examples of different types of graphs, charts, and visual organizations of data, all intended to communicate specific information about a group or topic. It is important that students have some facility with looking at and using different representations so that they too can make sense out of the information presented and be critical readers of data.

Attending to Important Features of the Data Such as the Range and the Mode When looking at a graph, young students quite naturally are drawn to the mode—the point with the most data. In addition, they are interested in the highest and lowest data values. Questions like What's the fewest number of teeth lost by a fourth grader? and What's the largest number of pockets worn by someone in our class? lead students to gather some important information about a data set. Although most young students are not ready to engage in more sophisticated types of comparisons, this early experience, interest, and attention to features of the data can provide interesting and important information and form the basis for their future work with data.

Using Data Representations as a Way of Communicating Information In some elementary classrooms, graphs are viewed as artwork rather than tools for communicating information. By involving students in describing data representations (e.g., What's the overall shape of the data?) and what sorts of things they can learn about a group based on how the data are organized, they begin to experience how a graph tells a story. Graphs are active tools, and students need to be actively involved in their creation and interpretation.

Any data investigation generally includes recognizable phases:

- considering the problem (choosing a question to investigate)
- collecting and recording data
- organizing the data
- representing the data
- describing and interpreting the data
- developing hypotheses and theories based on the data

These phases often occur in a cycle: the development of a theory based on the data often leads to a new question, which may begin the data analysis cycle all over again. In this unit, students engage in all aspects of data analysis.

Mathematical Emphasis At the beginning of each investigation, the Mathematical Emphasis section tells you what is most important for students to learn about during that investigation. Many of these understandings and processes are difficult and complex. Students gradually learn more and more about each idea over many years of schooling. Individual students will begin and end the unit with different levels of knowledge and skill, but all will gain greater knowledge about how to collect, organize, represent, describe, and interpret data.

In the *Investigations* curriculum, mathematical vocabulary is introduced naturally during the activities. We don't ask students to learn definitions of new terms; rather, they come to understand such words as *data, graph, area,* and *symmetry* by hearing them used frequently in discussion as they investigate new concepts. This approach is compatible with current theories of second-language acquisition, which emphasize the use of new vocabulary in meaningful contexts while students are actively involved with objects, pictures, and physical movement.

Listed below are some key words used in this unit that will not be new to most English speakers at this age level but may be unfamiliar to students with limited English proficiency. You will want to spend additional time working on these words with your students who are learning English. If your students are working with a second-language teacher, you might enlist your colleague's aid in familiarizing students with these words before and during this unit. In the classroom, look for opportunities for students to hear and use these words. Activities you can use to present the words are given in the appendix, Vocabulary Support for Second-Language Learners (p. 97).

age, how old, younger, older   Students look at various age groups as they collect data throughout this unit, and use age to categorize some data.

siblings, brothers, sisters   One data collection project includes investigating how many *siblings* students have.

organize, order   Throughout this unit, students will be working to organize the data they collect, then create representations to display the data.

lost, missing   Students need to make some distinctions between the terms missing and lost as they collect data and create representations.

Multicultural Extensions for All Students

Whenever possible, encourage students to share words, objects, customs, or any aspects of daily life from their own cultures and backgrounds that are relevant to the activities in this unit. For example:

- Ask students to describe what they do in their home when they lose a tooth. For example, some students may say they place it under their beds or pillows at night. Encourage students from various cultural backgrounds to tell about their expeiences.

- Ask students to describe any special clothing that represents cultural dress and if the clothing has any pockets. If so, ask students to think about what the purpose of the pockets might be.

Investigations

Exploring Numerical Data

What Happens

Session 1: Quick Data Collections   The class works together to create different types of graphs in response to numerical data questions posed by the teacher.

Sessions 2 and 3: Pocket Towers   Students answer survey questions for use in Sessions 4 and 5. Then they collect data by building towers that represent the number of pockets they are wearing. Together they discuss ways to organize these pocket towers. Each pair of students organizes a class set of pocket towers to create their own representation of the class pocket data. They draw a picture of their representation.

Sessions 4 and 5: Class Surveys   Pairs of students choose one of the survey questions that they answered in Session 2 to investigate further. Students organize and represent a class set of survey data from one question. They share their representations in groups, then discuss systems for keeping track with the whole class.

Mathematical Emphasis

- Collecting data
- Keeping track of data
- Organizing numerical data
- Creating representations
- Seeing representations as a way of communicating to others
- Describing and interpreting representations

What to Plan Ahead of Time

Materials

- Inch graph paper (Session 1)
- Student math folders: 1 per student (Session 1)
- Chart paper (Sessions 1–3)
- Scissors, markers, tape (Sessions 1–5)
- Plastic bags or shoe boxes: 1 per group (Sessions 2 and 3)
- Large paper: 2–3 per student (Sessions 2–5)
- Interlocking cubes: class set (Sessions 2–5)
- Color tiles or other manipulatives: class sets (Sessions 4 and 5)
- Class list of names: 2–3 per student (Sessions 2–5)

Other Preparation

For Session 1

- Duplicate Student Sheet 1, Weekly Log, 1 per student. At this time, you may wish to duplicate a supply to last for the entire unit and distribute the sheets as needed. Prepare a math folder for each student if you haven't done so previously.
- Prepare the Number of Letters in Our Name graph by taping two pieces of chart paper together horizontally. You will need to create a range from 0 to 10 (or more) depending on the names in your class. The numbers on the graph will not be evenly spaced. Since the length of the graph paper strips that students will be posting will vary, the placement of numbers on the graph should reflect this. Cut strips of graph paper 1 box to 10 boxes and use these as a guide for measuring how much space to leave.
- Cut inch graph paper into strips. To determine the length of each strip, allow one box per letter and make all strips as long as the longest name in the class. If a name like Stephanie is the longest name, prepare a 1"-by-9" strip for each student.

For Sessions 2 and 3

- Duplicate Student Sheet 2, Surveys, 1 per pair. Cut apart the student sheets, providing 1 survey form to each student.
- Prepare a class list of names and duplicate 1 per student.
- Prepare a class list of names on chart paper. The order of the names should match those on the student list.
- If you have previously have used an *Investigations* unit and have gathered Pocket Data, display it again for discussion during this session.
- Duplicate the Family letter (p. 100), 1 per family. Remember to sign and date the letter before copying.

For Sessions 4 and 5

- Duplicate the class list of names, 1 per pair.
- Gather students' completed Student Sheets 2, and duplicate 1 class set per pair.

Quick Data Collections

Materials

- Chart paper
- Prepared graph: Number of Letters in Our Name
- Inch graph paper cut into strips (1 per student)
- Student Sheet 1 (1 per student)
- Math folders (1 per student)
- Scissors, markers, tape

What Happens

The class works together to create different types of graphs in response to numerical data questions posed by the teacher. Their work focuses on :

- collecting numerical data
- representing class data in a variety of ways
- developing language to interpret data

Start-Up

Today's Number Today's Number is one of three routines that are built into the grade 2 *Investigations* curriculum. Routines provide students regular practice in important mathematical ideas such as number combinations, counting and estimating data, and concepts of time. For Today's Number, which is done daily (or most days), students write number sentences that equal the number of days they have been in school. The complete description of Today's Number (pp. 88–90), offers suggestions for establishing this routine and some variations.

If you are doing the full-year grade 2 *Investigations* curriculum, you will have already started a 200 chart and a counting strip during the unit *Mathematical Thinking at Grade 2*. Write the next number on the 200 chart and add the next number card to the counting strip. As a class, brainstorm ways to express the number.

If you are teaching an *Investigations* unit for the first time, here are a few options for incorporating Today's Number as a routine:

- **Begin with 1** Begin a counting line that does not correspond to the school day number. Each day add a number to the strip and use this number as Today's Number.
- **Use the Calendar Date** If today is the sixteenth day of the month, use 16 as Today's Number.

After Today's Number has been established, ask students to think about different ways to write the number. Post a piece of chart paper to record their suggestions. You might want to offer ideas to help students get started. If Today's Number is 45, you might suggest 40 + 5 or 20 + 25.

Ask students to think about other ways to make Today's Number. List their suggestions on chart paper. As students offer suggestions, occasionally ask the group if they agree with the statements. This gives students the opportunity to confirm an idea that they had or to respond to an incorrect suggestion.

As students grow accustomed to this routine, they will begin to see patterns in the combinations, have favorite kinds of number sentences, or use more complicated types of expressions. Today's Number can be recorded daily on the Weekly Log. (See p. 24.)

(See p. 24.)

How Old Are the Kids in Our Class?

Students will be working for the next few weeks with the topic of data. See the **Teacher Note,** What Are Data, Anyway? (p. 25), for more information about collecting and interpreting data. If you have explored data and created graphs with students before, you may want to point out some graphs around the room or ask students what they remember about collecting data.

For the next few weeks in our math class, we'll be collecting information or data about each other, about students in our school, and about our families.

Mathematicians and scientists use data to help them understand the world, to compare things, and to keep track of things. What are some kinds of data we've collected this year already? What other data or information have we kept track of?

If you are doing the full-year *Investigations* curriculum, students may recall data collection experiences from the units *Mathematical Thinking at Grade 2* and *Does It Walk, Crawl, or Swim?*, such as Guess My Rule activities and Sink and Float experiments. They may recall Today's Number and Pocket Day as other events to keep track of. Perhaps you keep track of lunch orders or attendance.

We'll be looking at different ways to collect data, to organize them, to show or make representations of data, and to make sense of whatever data we collect. Representations are things like pictures, graphs, tables, and charts that show the data. By the end of the unit, you'll have a chance to think of a question that you'd like to find out more about and collect your own data.

There are different kinds of data that people collect. We're going to be exploring numerical data, which usually answers the question "How many?" *Numerical* **comes from the word** *number.* **All the answers to our questions will be in numbers. For example, instead of asking, "What kind of pet do you have?," we could ask, "How many pets do you have?"**

If you've already done the unit *Does It Walk, Crawl, or Swim?* you might want to make the comparison between numerical and categorical data more explicit. Students will have a chance to explore the question "How many pets do you have?" during Sessions 2 and 3.

Today we're going to make a few different graphs together. The first one we'll make is a people graph to find out how old the kids in this class are. About how old do you think the kids in this class are? What's the range of possibilities?

As students share ideas about the range of the data, some may say, "between 7 and 9," or they may give a specific number like, "I'm 8." When all the possible answers are collected on the board, you may want to check by asking, "Is anyone a different age from what is already written here?" Then write the range of possible ages in order from left to right on the board, for example:

---

                    7   8   9

Students who are on the younger or older end may be sensitive about their age. See the **Teacher Note,** Dealing with Sensitive Issues: But I Haven't Lost a Tooth Yet (p. 52).

This quick data collection works best if *you* decide on answers to controversial questions that arise (as opposed to discussing it with the class), since you are the one posing the questions. For example, students may say that they are 7½, or that they are 7 but their birthday is next week, so they are closer to 8. You might decide, for example, that both of these students should consider themselves 7, as that is their current age.

Students in this class are between 7 and 9 years old. That's the *range* of possible ages. In this class, you're either 7, 8, or 9. Anyone who is 7, come stand in a line here [*in front of the 7 on the board***]. If you're 8, line up in front of the 8 [***on the board***]. OK, now the 9-year-olds come on up.**

Have students face away from the chalkboard so they can see the general form of the graph.

- **What do you notice about our graph?**
- **Which line is the longest? What does that mean?**
- **How many students in this class are 8?**
- **If we had made this graph at the beginning of the year, what might be different? How might the shape of our graph look?**

This should be a brief discussion, since students may have a hard time seeing the overall shape of the graph while they are in it. The main purpose is for students to experience the graphing process and how a graph provides information. As a class, determine the number of students in each age category. Record this information on the board by writing a sentence such as, "10 children are 7 years old."

How many years old are you?

7   8   9

How Many Siblings Do We Have?

Tell students that you want to find out how many brothers and sisters everyone has. Write "How many siblings do you have?" on the chalkboard or chart paper and explain that the next set of data that you'll be collecting is about siblings.

Siblings is a word that means "brothers and sisters." If I were answering this question about my siblings, I'd say that I have one because of my brother, Daniel. I don't include myself in this count. So even though there are two children in my family, I have one sibling.

You can decide whom to count (half-brothers, siblings who don't live with you) as long as you don't count yourself.

Last time we made a people graph to keep track of the data we collected. This time we'll keep track of the information we collect by using a *line plot*. First I want to write the range of possible responses. What do you think the lowest possible number of siblings we have could be? What about the highest possible number? Now we'll put an X on the line plot to show how many siblings each of us has.

Use the lowest and highest numbers to establish the range on your line plot. Add at least one number below the smallest number (unless it's zero) and one number above the largest to show that there are other possible amounts. Here is an example of a line plot showing the number of siblings.

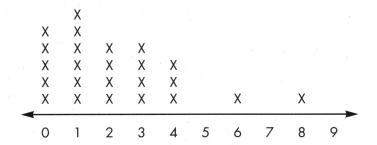

Ask each student how many siblings he or she has and record an X above that number. This method of recording allows students to see their individual data represented. You might ask students to tell you where they think their X should go. Continue until the graph is complete.

How could we check to make sure we've included everyone?

Students may suggest writing names or initials next to the X's as a way of checking (or even as a way of completing the graph). Or you might simply decide to check by looking at each number represented.

How many students do we have in class today? So how many X's do you think there should be? [*Someone counts.*] **Looking at the line plot, can you tell how many students have 2 siblings? Raise your hand if you have 2 siblings.**

Students compare the number of X's to the number of students raising their hands. If these numbers do not correspond, students determine the correct number and the graph is revised.

What do you notice about our sibling data from looking at the line plot?

Students might comment on the frequency of certain numbers, for example, "3 people have 4 siblings"; the number of siblings had by the most number of people, "1 is the highest"; or what the line plot looks like, "It is tall and then gets smaller like stairs going down."

Ask students to compare certain data, such as the number of students who have 2 siblings to those who have no siblings. Save this sibling representation and move on to another quick data collection.

How Many Letters in Our Names?

Distribute a strip of inch graph paper to each student and explain that the class is going to make a representation of the number of letters in students' names. Tell students they will post their data on a chart titled "Number of Letters in Our Names."

Each student should write his or her name on the graph-paper strip, putting one letter in each box. Remind students to hold the paper horizontally. They'll need to cut off the excess paper; for example, if a name has five letters, the paper strip should be exactly five boxes (inches) long. Students can choose nicknames or whole names.

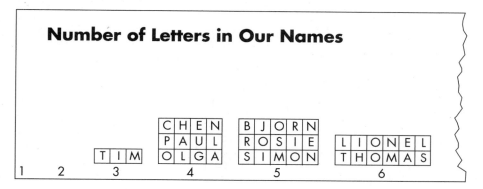

After students have written their names, have them tape their strips above the appropriate number on the graph.

- **What do you notice about this graph?**
- **What can we say about the number of letters in our names?**
- **How long are most names in our class?**
- **We collect data to help us find information out for different purposes. How could these data be useful information?**

Students might suggest that knowing the length of student names could be useful for a variety of purposes such as making name tags for desks. See the **Teacher Note**, What Are Data, Anyway? (p. 25), for more information about reasons for collecting data.

Introducing Math Folders and Weekly Logs

If you are using the full-year *Investigations* curriculum, students will be familiar with math folders and Weekly Logs. If this curriculum is new to students, tell them about one way they will keep track of their math work.

Mathematicians show how they think about and solve problems by talking about their work, drawing pictures, building models, and explaining their work in writing so that they can share their ideas with other people. Your math folder will be a place to collect the writing and drawing that you do in math class.

Distribute math folders to students and have them label the folders with their names.

Your math folder is a place to keep track of what you do each day in math class. Sometimes there will be more than one activity to choose from, and at other times, like today, everyone in the class will do the same thing. Each day you will record what you did on this Weekly Log.

Distribute Student Sheet 1, Weekly Log, and ask students to write their names at the top of the page. Point out that there are spaces for each day of the week and ask them to write today's date on the line after the appropriate day. If you are doing the activity Today's Number, students can write the number in the box beside the date.

Ask for suggestions about what to call today's activities. Titles for choices and whole-class activities should be short, to encourage all students to record what they do each day. List their ideas on the board and let students choose one title to write in the space below the date.

❖ **Tip for the Linguistically Diverse Classroom** Encourage students who are not writing comfortably in English to use drawings to record in their Weekly Log. If students demonstrate some proficiency in writing, suggest that they record a few words with their drawings. Students can also record a sample problem representative of each day's work.

Weekly Logs can be stapled to the front of the folders (each new week on the top so prior logs can be viewed by lifting up the sheets).

During the unit (or throughout the year), you might use the math folders and Weekly Logs in a number of ways:

- to keep track of what kinds of activities students choose to do and how frequently they choose them
- to review with students, individually or as a group, the work they've accomplished
- to share student work with families, by sending folders home periodically for students to share or during student/family/teacher conferences

What Are Data, Anyway?

I'm 48 inches tall and my brother is 58 inches tall.

This bottle holds 2 liters of soda pop.

Most people in our class are wearing sneakers.

These shoes weigh 150 grams.

Each of these statements contains descriptive information or data about some person or thing. Data are the facts, or the information, that differentiate and describe people, objects, or other entities. Data may be expressed as numbers (he is 48 inches tall; she has 4 people in her family) or as attributes (her favorite flavor is chocolate; his hair is curly).

Data are collected through surveys, observation, measuring, counting, and experiments. If we study rainfall, we might collect rain and measure the amount that falls each day. If we study hair color, we might observe and record the color of each person's hair.

Collecting data involves detailed judgments about how to count, measure, or describe. Should we record rainfall data for each day or for each rainstorm? Should we round off to the nearest inch? Should we count just one color for a person's hair? Should we record "yellow" or "dirty blond" or "gold"? Should "brown" be a single category, or should it be divided into several shades?

Once data are collected, recorded, counted, and analyzed, we can use them as the basis for making decisions. In one school, a study of accidents on a particular piece of playground equipment showed that most of the accidents involved children who were in the first, second, and third grades. Those who studied the data realized that the younger students' hands were too small to grasp the bars firmly enough. A decision to keep primary grade children off this equipment was made because the data, or the facts, led to that conclusion.

When students collect data, they are collecting information. When they interpret these data, they are developing theories or generalizations. The data provide the basis for their theories.

Pocket Towers

Materials

- Interlocking cubes (class set)
- Chart paper
- Large paper (1 per student)
- Previous pocket data results or representations (if available)
- Class lists of names (1 per student)
- Bags or boxes to store cube towers
- Pencils, markers
- Student Sheet 2 (1 per pair)
- Family letter (1 per family)

What Happens

Students answer survey questions for use in Sessions 4 and 5. Then they collect data by building towers that represent the number of pockets they are wearing. Together they discuss ways to organize these pocket towers. Each pair of students organizes a class set of pocket towers to create their own representation of the class pocket data. They draw a picture of their representation. Their work focuses on:

- exploring ways to organize numerical data
- creating a representation of pocket data
- keeping track of data

Start-Up

Today's Number

- **Calendar Date**   If you are using the calendar date for Today's Number, brainstorm with students ways to express the number. Suggest that they include subtraction in their expression. Record students' expressions on chart paper so that they can be saved each day.

- **Number of School Days**   If you are using the number of school days as Today's Number, and the number is over 100, encourage students to focus on ways to make 100 using multiples of 5 and 10. For example, if the number is 142, one solution is 35 + 25 + 25 + 20 + 20 + 10 + 5 + 2. Add a card to the class counting strip and fill in another number on the blank 200 chart.

Activity

Surveys

During this session, or before Session 4, introduce the class survey.

We are going to be taking a survey of our class. Has anyone ever been part of a survey or do you know someone who has been?

Distribute the survey questions on Student Sheet 2, Surveys, to each pair of students. (Cut the Student Sheet apart so each student has a survey sheet.) As a class, read each of the survey questions aloud and ask students why they think some of these questions might be interesting to explore. This also gives students a chance to clarify the meaning of a particular question.

Tip for the Linguistically Diverse Classroom To make each survey question clear to students with limited English proficiency, draw rebuses to represent the question, or point to examples. Students can also draw their own rebuses above each corresponding word on Student Sheet 2.

Students answer the questions on their survey forms. Their answers should be in numerals, but some students may find it easier to draw pictures. Remind students to write their numbers clearly so that someone else can read them. They may put their names on their survey forms if they like, but as in many adult surveys, this is optional.

Explain to students that in a few days they will analyze the data they just collected. Collect the surveys and copy one complete class set for each pair of students.

Introducing Pocket Towers

Introduce this data collection activity by explaining that you'll be collecting pocket data from the whole class. If you are using the full-year *Investigations* curriculum (or if you've done the pocket routine in another unit), students will be familiar with counting pockets. Instead of focusing on the total number of pockets, students organize the data by grouping the towers so they can see how many are wearing certain numbers of pockets.

We are going to take a survey to find how many pockets each of you is wearing. We will collect this information and then organize it so we can compare how many pockets you have on.

We're going to make cube towers to keep track of the information. I'm wearing 4 pockets, so I'll put 4 cubes in my tower.

Each student makes a tower that shows how many pockets he or she is wearing. Students bring these to a central location that all can see, such as the middle of the circle on the floor or the chalkboard ledge.

The issue of how to represent zero pockets will probably arise. This issue is mentioned in the **Teacher Note**, What Do Students' Invented Representations Look Like? (p. 32). You will have to decide with students how to show zero pockets. What's most important is that students do what makes sense to them as a group. Resolving this may involve a short discussion. Some classes have used stick-on notes or a different-color cube to keep track of the number of people with zero pockets.

Record each student's name and the number of pockets on chart paper. (It may be helpful to have the names on chart paper and the small class lists in the same order for keeping track later in the session when students create their own set of pocket data.)

Harris, put your tower here and tell us how many pockets you're wearing. I'm going to record on paper how many pockets each person is wearing.

When the towers have been collected, ask students to think about the correspondence between the number of students and the number of towers. These may differ, as some students may have had zero pockets. Students with zero pockets might be represented with something like a black cube, or a stick-on note, if the class agrees that this makes sense to them.

How many towers do you think we have here?

Students make predictions, then count the towers. Ask students about what the towers mean.

- **What does this tower of 4 cubes show?**
- **What does each cube stand for?**
- **How many people have two pockets?**
- **Can we tell from these towers how many people have zero pockets?**

You'll be working with partners to organize a set of towers just like these. What are some ways to organize these pocket towers so we can see how many people are wearing the same number of pockets?

If students don't understand what *organize* means, ask them to think about which ones go together, or how they could group the cube towers. Some students may suggest organizing the towers by putting them in order. Others may be thinking about color. Encourage them to explain why they would group in a particular way and invite them to try part of it.

Keep in mind that this is a brainstorming session so that students have some ways to begin their work with partners. It is not necessary to have students demonstrate their idea with the entire set of pocket towers. Students may be able to show what they mean by grouping a few towers together and explaining the rest of their plan. See the **Dialogue Box,** Describing and Organizing Pocket Towers (p. 34).

Creating a Pocket Representation

Work with a partner to make a class set of pocket towers to match the set we have here. You can use this class list I have been writing on to help you know what to build. Use a copy of our class list to help you keep track of which towers you have built. How many towers do you think you should have when you're done building?

When you have built a class set of cube towers, organize them in some way, then draw a picture to show your work.

You may need to remind students about the situation regarding those with zero pockets. These students may not have a cube tower, or they may have represented zero pockets in another way.

Provide each pair with interlocking cubes and a class list of names. Students may need to work in small groups, depending on the amount of interlocking cubes that are available.

When students seem clear on the task, have them begin. It may help if you write the directions on paper:

1. Make a class set of pocket towers.

2. Organize the pocket towers.

3. Draw a picture of your representation.

You may want to end Session 2 after students have finished making their set of pocket towers. Use bags, shoe boxes, or baskets to store the towers. Remind students to label their class lists with a title like "Pocket Data" since they will be using many class lists in this unit.

At the beginning of Session 3, spend a few minutes asking students to remind one another about ways they might organize their class set of towers. If you noticed some clear organization methods that students used, ask those students to share what they did. See the **Teacher Note**, What Is a Representation? (p. 31), for a discussion on *representations*.

It is important to give students enough time to explore ways of organizing their own data. After students have organized their pocket towers, they'll need large paper for drawing their representations.

About 15 minutes before the end of Session 3, remind students that they should choose one way of organizing the towers and draw a representation of what they've done. If they finish early, ask them to clarify their representation so that someone else could understand it. You can also have students begin the homework problem: How many pockets is our class wearing?

Observing the Students

As students are working on organizing and representing the data, circulate and observe their work.

- How do students keep track of the data? Do they use the class list? Do they check to see if everyone's data are represented? Do they check to see if the data on their graph correspond to the number of people who contributed information?
- Can you tell by looking how they've organized their representation?
- (How) do they represent the people with zero pockets?
- How have students chosen to organize the data? What aspect of the data is important in their representation? Which towers do they think belong together and why?
- (How) do they group the data? (How) do they order the data?

If a representation is unclear, you may ask one of the following questions to gain insight into students' thinking and possibly to help them clarify their ideas:

- **Can you tell me how you are showing the number of pockets people are wearing?**
- **How many pockets are you wearing? Is anyone else wearing the same number as you are? Can you show me all the people who are wearing [4] pockets?**
- **What can someone learn about the pockets in our class from looking at this graph?**

Students' explanations can give you a sense of whether their chosen way to represent the data makes sense to them. Quite likely there will be representations that do not make sense to you. Representations may communicate parts of the data gathered that are important to a student. The ability to organize and represent data develops over time, with multiple opportunities both to do it and observe how others do it. Allow representations to stand if they make sense to a student.

In the last 10 minutes of Session 3, invite students to reflect on their first experience organizing numerical data.

How did you organize your towers? What does [Jess's] recording tell you about pockets in our class?

Note: Students should finish filling out their surveys by the end of Session 3, so that you have time to photocopy the class set of survey data for Session 4. You'll need 1 copy of each completed student survey form for each student.

Sessions 2 and 3 Follow-Up

- Ask students to solve this problem for homework: How many pockets is our class wearing? If you are doing the full-year *Investigations* curriculum, students will be familiar with this problem. Students need a class list with the number of pockets for each student recorded on it. (They may have this from earlier in the session, or you may want to photocopy these data for their instructions.) Ask students to use words, numbers, and/or pictures to record how they figured out the total number of pockets in the class.

- Send home the Family letter, one for each family.

🏠 Homework

Collecting Pocket Data from Older Students   Pocket data sessions can be extended by collecting pocket data from older students. Second grade students predict what the range of pockets might be and what they expect the data to look like. As they make their predictions, ask them to think about whether older students dress differently from second graders. Then they collect, organize, and represent the data in a way that is similar to the teeth activities in Investigation 2, Sessions 3–5.

▨ Extension

What Is a Representation?

Teacher Note

What is a representation? One student said that it means "to show the data." Creating representations of data is something that may be new to students. At first this may seem challenging, but keep in mind that skill in organizing and representing data develops over time with experience.

One important goal is for students to consider their representations a form of communication. Thus, graphing is not simply a set of rules that one learns. Thinking about what the data mean as a way to inform yourself and/or someone else about the subject may be a new way to think about graphing and symbolization. When students have a chance to explore data, they encounter for themselves the many problems that creators of conventional graphs have attempted to deal with. Through revising representations, and through further exploration of data, students' representations will become more consistent.

Interpreting data is a way to focus on what a representation tells you. What is the "story" the author is trying to tell? If the information is about something that students have had experience with, they may have some intuitive sense of what to expect even before they collect any data. One second grader was very surprised that her cousin had lost seven teeth in kindergarten, since most of the kindergartners she knows haven't lost any teeth.

In this unit, students briefly look at "teacher-organized" graphs and quickly begin creating their own representations of data. In the final project of the unit, students are involved in all aspects of data collection and representation, including generating their own questions, deciding how to collect data, and representing those data.

As students begin to organize and represent data, it is important to be supportive of what they are representing rather than focus on what is missing or not represented. Don't expect that every student will create the same graph or that they will create conventional bar graphs. When looking at an unconventional representation, even if it is not immediately clear, presume that the student has represented some aspect of the data that is important to him or her. If a graph is unclear, ask the author what he or she was trying to show. By pointing out what a graph tells you, you emphasize the idea of graphing as an activity that communicates information to others.

Second grade students tend to produce data-driven representations. That is, they consider only the data they have, rather than include places on their representation for other potential responses. For example, in the pizza graph at the right, the students have not filled in all the numbers within the range (i.e., from 0 to 8). They simply recorded the information that they had available, leaving out the rest. To these students it was unimportant that nobody in their class ate six or seven pieces of pizza, although they may infer this later from looking at the graph.

Another factor common to many young students' representations is grouping the data but not arranging it in order. The pizza graph is also an example of data that have been grouped (all the 1's together, all the 2's together) but not ordered. Without putting the data in order from 0 to 8, students can still look at the graph and see, for example, that most people eat three pieces of pizza. These students grouped their data along a baseline (starting from the top), though sometimes students group data in clumps or piles, rather than along a line.

As students begin to represent numerical data, do not expect all numbers in the range to be filled in or the data to be grouped and ordered.

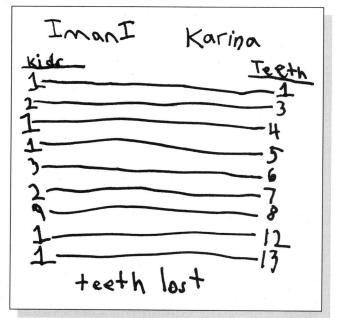

The data below are represented like a number table. Data are grouped and ordered. As in the pizza graph above, not all numbers in the range have been included. A question for students might be, "If you talked to another second grade class, where would you record the data for a person who has lost two teeth?"

Continued on next page

This next graph is an example of data that are ordered. It communicates information visually as well. At a glance we can see that a lot of people were wearing five or six pockets and one person was wearing a lot of pockets. This student did not choose to represent those who had zero pockets, so the graph does not represent the data from the entire class. By simply counting the bars, we can see how many people were wearing at least one pocket.

In the pets representation below the students apparently considered it important information that many classmates have no pets. They chose to represent these people. Although the data are grouped and ordered, this graph is more like a list.

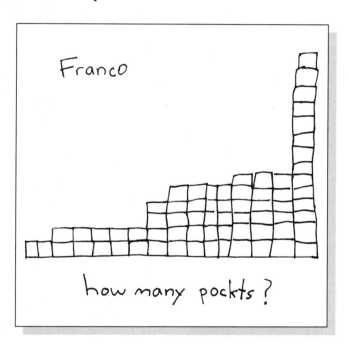

Franco

how many pockts ?

Helena   Ebony

PETS

0000 0000 |||||| 2 2

33   44   5   6   8

┌D┐┌I┐┌A┐┌L┐┌O┐┌G┐┌U┐┌E┐ ┌B┐┌O┐┌X┐

Describing and Organizing Pocket Towers

In this conversation, which occurred as students organized their pocket towers (p. 29), the teacher helps students focus on ways of describing and grouping data. The teacher has asked students to create a tower that shows how many pockets they have on and place it along an imaginary line in the center of the rug. Since some students had zero pockets, they did not make a tower. The result is a series of towers that looks like this:

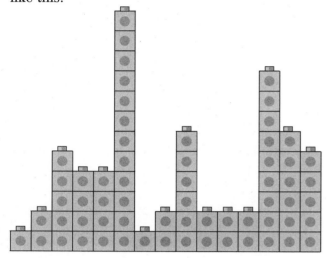

What do you notice about these data?

Laura: From this way [*where she's sitting*] it looks like a city.

Juanita: It looks like Boston. Or New York. And this would be the Hancock Tower [*points to the tallest cube tower*].

A really tall building!

Lila: Carla's tower is *way* bigger than any of them. Are we going to put them in order of how many?

What do other people notice?

Laura: It's like New York and this [*pointing to the tallest tower*] is the Empire State Building. We're missing the Twin Towers.

What do you notice about the numbers?

Olga: It looks sort of like 1 then 2, then up higher [*looking at the towers in order from left to right.*] There were a lot of people that had 2.

Phoebe: If this and this, were the same color, [*pointing to 2 towers that were each 6 high*] then they could be the Twin Towers.

Because they are the same height.

Harris: Mine's like Phoebe's. If there were 4 Twin Towers these could be them [*holding up 4 towers that are each 2 high*]. And the clouds would be right here [*pointing to the rug near the tall tower*]. And the 1's are the smallest buildings in New York.

Juanita: Like little hotels!

Jess: The Twin Towers aren't tall enough; they'd have to be up to here [*just below 12 on the tallest tower*].

Lionel: They're data, not buildings. I think the 1's go here, the 2's, then the 3's here.

So you want to organize them like Lila [*in order of how many*]?

Franco: You could have the tallest and then the sort of tallest and then have it like a staircase.

OK. In partners you'll make a set of towers like these, and I want you to arrange them. Let's leave out the city idea for now. Think about the numbers and groups. What would go together?

Lila: My idea is sort of like Franco's. You could have 12, then the next biggest [9], then find the next biggest [*takes two 6's*].

So you would put them in order from tallest to shortest. How about another way?

Olga: Do like 1, 2, 3, 4, and go up.

So instead of tallest to shortest, do shortest to tallest? OK. Do you know another way to make piles or stacks?

Continued on next page

Carla: Put the tallest aside [*places 12 and 9 aside together*]. Then take the smallest ones [*takes the 2's and 1's and puts them near each other*]. Then take the middle-size ones. [*She places 6's in one scattered pile and the 5's and 4's in another. She has four piles spread around the rug.*]

Harris: Mine is like Carla's, but not just like it. [*He takes the four piles and puts them in order from smallest to tallest leaving the four groupings separated from each other.*]

During this conversation, students attend to visual aspects of the cube towers by describing the towers as buildings in a skyline. They look at significant features of the data by describing, for example, one tower of 12 as "the Hancock" or "the Empire State Building." Your students will make different connections.

The teacher acknowledges these comments but encourages students to focus on the numbers and on making groups. Some students work with the idea of ordering the data (tallest to shortest, shortest to tallest), and others consider grouping the data, thus creating ranges (1–2, 4–5, 6, 9–12). The shared language of buildings that led to a discussion of the heights of towers using numbers supported students in organizing the towers based on their visual observations of the data.

Sessions 4 and 5

Class Surveys

Materials

- Copies of completed Student Sheet 2 (1 class set per pair)
- Large paper (1–2 per pair)
- Class lists of names (1 per pair)
- Interlocking cubes, color tiles, or paper squares for representing data

What Happens

Pairs of students choose one of the survey questions that they answered in Session 2 to investigate further. Students organize and represent a class set of survey data from one question. They share their representations in groups, then discuss systems for keeping track with the whole class. Their work focuses on:

- keeping track of the data
- creating a representation
- interpreting representations

Start-Up

Today's Number

- **Calendar Date** If you are using the calendar for Today's Number, work with students to brainstorm ways to express the number using combinations of 10. For example, if the number they are working on is 23 and one number sentence is $10 + 10 + 3$, ask students if there is another way of making 10, such as $(6 + 4) + (6 + 4) + 3$ or $(4 + 3 + 2 + 1) + (4 + 3 + 2 + 1) + 3$. Record their expressions on chart paper.

- **Number of School Days** If you are using the number of school days for Today's Number, work with students to brainstorm ways to express the number using both addition and subtraction. For example, if the number is 145, possible solutions are $200 - 100 + 45$ and $100 + 50 - 5$. Add a card to the class counting strip and fill in another number on the blank 200 chart.

How Many Pockets? Ask students to share some of their strategies from last night's homework for adding the total number of pockets worn in class.

Activity

Teacher Checkpoint

Creating a Representation

Teacher checkpoints are places for you to stop and observe students and their work. This checkpoint is an opportunity to look carefully at how students are thinking about and organizing data.

Distribute a class set of completed Student Sheet 2, Survey, to each pair of students. (Responses were completed during Sessions 2 and 3.) Display cubes, color tiles, or any other material that students can use to make their representation.

Each pair has the whole class's response to all four survey questions. You and your partner should choose one of these questions that interests you. Then you will make a representation that shows the class's answers to your question.

When you've chosen a question, you'll need to figure out what kind of representation you'd like to make and how you'll keep track of the data as you work.

Record the directions on paper while you are talking:

1. Choose one question.

2. Create a representation.

3. Keep track.

4. Draw your representation.

Students may initially use cubes, paper squares, tiles, sketches, or other materials to create a representation that shows the entire class's response to a particular question. Make these available and remind students that they will need to re-create their representations on paper to save for later use. Then they may put away their other materials. Brainstorm some procedural suggestions together.

What are some ways you could show the information about one question? How will you organize your information?

Students also share a few ideas for keeping track. Since there are lots of papers to work with, it's easy to get confused about which ones students have already looked at and recorded and which ones they haven't. Some students may suggest putting the sheets in different groups. Others may suggest turning the sheets over. Some may want to make check marks on the survey responses that they've used. Students should do what makes sense to them. See the **Teacher Note**, Keeping Track of Data (p. 40), for more information about students' methods for keeping track.

Explain to students that they will work on these representations for the rest of this session as well as the first part of the following session. At the end of tomorrow's session, they'll share their representation and discuss their system for keeping track.

Observing the Students

As students are working, use the following questions to guide your observations:

■ How do students keep track of the data?

■ How do they organize the data? In what ways do they group the data?

■ What does their representation communicate about the data?

■ What interests them about a certain question?

■ What observations can they make about their data?

■ Can students find themselves in their representations?

All students' graphs are attempts to communicate something about the data that is significant to them. During this unit you'll want to ask students to clarify parts of their representation that are unclear to you. One important goal is that students use and see representations as ways to communicate information. See the **Teacher Note**, What Do Students' Invented Representations Look Like? (p. 31), for more information about interpreting students' work.

Remind students that at the end of Session 4, they'll need to write on their representations what their representation shows (example: "How many pieces of pizza our class eats for dinner"). If they have used class lists, suggest that they label them with the same heading.

If students finish early they should write three interesting things they observed about the data or share their representation with another pair.

Class Discussion: Different Ways to Represent the Data

Leave about 20 to 30 minutes at the end of Session 5 for students to share their paper and pencil representations. It is suggested that you organize this discussion by going over one survey question at a time. This will enable students to look across representations of the same data and compare them.

Those of you who worked on the shoelace question come to the front of the room with your representation. What do you notice about these that is similar? What's different about them? What can you tell about the number of shoelace holes in our class from this one? How about from this one? What do you suppose this X stands for? What surprised you?

Some of the students who are sharing shoelace representations can tell about the ways they kept track. You may want to focus on a pair whose representation hasn't gotten much attention yet. You might:

- ask students to show the paper on which they kept track of their work (class list, for example) and to explain why they think they have included all responses.
- ask about how many pieces of data they have in all.
- ask about the shape of the data.
- point out anything particularly interesting you notice in the representation.

Discuss each of the four survey questions. See the **Dialogue Box**, Sharing Survey Representations (p. 41). Most likely there will be a range of representations reflecting different ways of understanding the data. It is not expected that students' representations will be clear and accurate, yet aspects will probably be clear. Organizing data is challenging the first few times; familiarity with data increases with time and experience. The exploration of ideas encountered in creating groupings to make sense of the data is an important part of the work. This experience is more important than the final product.

Sessions 4 and 5 Follow-Up

The Pizza Problem Students work individually using their class set of survey data and/or the representations posted to figure out how many pieces of pizza the class could eat for dinner and (if appropriate) how many pizzas would have to be ordered if each pizza has eight slices. They record their strategies and solutions using pictures and words. This could also be done as homework, if the information from the survey sheet pizza question is distributed to all.

 **Extension**

One of the most difficult parts of data collection for students (and adults) is creating a logical way to keep track of the many pieces of data they are collecting or need to collect. Knowing whom you have counted and whom you still need to count is basic to any data collection activity. Although counting and keeping track of the data may seem like straightforward tasks to adults, it is not obvious to most young students. Questions such as, "Is everyone's data represented in this graph? How do you know?" and "If there are 26 people in our class, how many pocket towers should we have and why?" help students make connections between the set of data they are collecting and the set of people they are collecting data from and also shows them that there is a one-to-one correspondence between these two groups.

In addition to understanding the need for keeping track of information, students must be given the opportunity to develop systems for keeping track. There are probably many ways that you keep track of information in your classroom. Attendance and lunch counts are familiar contexts to students. As you complete these tasks each day, explain your system for recording the data and keeping track of who has been counted or not counted. In fact, you may want to turn the responsibility of these tasks over to students at some point!

Although we can model different systems for keeping track, when students are collecting and organizing data it is important not to insist that they use a particular system, just a system that makes sense to them. The following are some examples of how some second grade students kept track of the class survey data.

Ebony: In our group I looked at the survey and then I wrote down the data. Carla put a check on the survey so we would know that we did it, and then Ping turned the papers over.

Tim: We used the class list. We wrote the number next to the person's name and then crossed off the name. Then we could tell whether anyone was missing.

Lila: First we put all the papers into groups. We put all the people with the same number of shoelace holes together. Then we counted all the papers in each pile and added it up. But it was 26 instead of 30 because there are 30 kids in the class. So we did it again and found out that we added wrong.

When students are given the opportunity to design and carry out their own data project (Investigation 3), keeping track of the data is just one aspect they must attend to. Don't be surprised if students who appeared to have developed some effective strategies for keeping track of the data forget to include that when they are planning their own data investigation. As they run into difficulty remembering whom they interviewed and whom they still need to interview, many will see the need to devise a method of keeping track.

Sharing Survey Representations

This discussion occurred when the teacher asked students to describe the ways they kept track of the data, how they organized them, and what their representations communicate about the data in the activity, Creating a Representation (p. 36). Pairs of students are sharing their representations from the survey question, "How many pieces of pizza do you usually eat for dinner?"

I would like you to tell us why you chose your question, how you kept track of your data, and how you organized and represented them.

Ping, Naomi, and Karina stand up.

Naomi: We chose pizza because we thought it would be kind of a lot of people who would eat a lot of slices. We found out that not very many people eat a lot of pieces.

Karina: We used cubes to help us figure it out.

So what did you do? Did one person read and another one write or . . . ?

Naomi: I looked at the survey, and then I wrote it down. Karina checked them off, Ping turned the papers over.

What does "4 = 0" mean?

Naomi: It means that 4 people don't like pizza.

Ayaz: We did the same one, but we got different information.

Interesting!

Ayaz: They got 4 zeros, we got 5. They put 1 for five, but we didn't get any, but we both got the same numbers [*total number of students*]. One person's answer was very messy and hard to read.

Naomi: When we were organizing it we kept on coming up with 21, then finally we got 22.

Did anyone else do pizza?

Linda, Olga, and Jeffrey stand up, and Ayaz notices right away that they also have 5 people for zero pizzas.

Linda: What we did was I read one, Jeffrey read one, and Olga wrote the numbers down. The reason I picked pizza is that a lot of people love pizza, so we thought the numbers would be hard.

Was anyone surprised?

Ayaz: I was surprised so many people didn't like pizza.

Lionel: I like pizza, but I never have it for dinner.

Bjorn: I like it too, but I've never had it for dinner.

Well, maybe the question should be changed. How could we rewrite the question so that it gives us the information we want?

During this sharing of representations students discovered that 0 doesn't necessarily mean that someone doesn't like pizza. This teacher then took the opportunity to discuss how to ask specific data questions, which is something that students will do more of in Investigation 3. This could have led to yet another survey, for example, "Do you like pizza?" and "Are you allowed to eat pizza for dinner?" in order to refine the data.

INVESTIGATION 2

Teeth Data

What Happens

Sessions 1 and 2: How Many Teeth Have You Lost? Students collect data that represent the number of teeth they have lost. They build a cube tower representation and make a line plot with stick-on notes, then compare these two representations of the data. Pairs of students create their own representations of the teeth data. At the end of Session 2, a class discussion focuses on different representations of the same data set. For homework, students collect data about the number of teeth lost by their siblings. This data will be used in Session 3.

Session 3: Comparing Lost Teeth Among Other Grades Students post the teeth data that they collected as homework. As a class they make and discuss predictions about collecting teeth data from other classes. In pairs they write or draw plans and organize materials so that they can collect data the following day.

Sessions 4 and 5: Collecting Teeth Data After a quick review of their data plans, pairs of students go to other classrooms to collect teeth data. They make a representation of these data using pencil and paper. They also use Student Sheet 5 as a guide for making sure their representation communicates certain information. At the end of Session 5, the class discusses their findings. This project is used as an assessment for students' understanding of collecting, organizing, and representing data.

Session 6: Mystery Teeth Data Students consider sets of Mystery Teeth Data collected from different grade levels. They create a pencil-and-paper representation of one set of data and exchange representations. Students then determine which set of Mystery Teeth Data their representation portrays. As a class they make hypotheses about which

grade level (K–4) the representations could represent based on the data, the representation, and their previous work with collecting teeth data from other classrooms.

Mathematical Emphasis

- Collecting numerical data
- Organizing and describing numerical data
- Focusing on important features of the data (range, unusual pieces of data)
- Representing the same data set using different materials
- Comparing data sets
- Interpreting data and making hypotheses based on data

What to Plan Ahead of Time

Materials

- *How Many Teeth?* by Paul Showers (Sessions 1 and 2, optional)
- Stick-on notes: 1–2 per student plus extras (Sessions 1 and 2)
- Master list of class names (Sessions 1 and 2)
- Class list of names: 1 per pair (Session 1)
- Large paper 12"-by-18" or larger: 2 per pair (Sessions 1 and 2, 4–6)
- Interlocking cubes: class set (Sessions 1–5)
- Square tiles: class set (Sessions 1–5)
- Assorted counters (Sessions 1–5)
- Index cards: about 20 (Session 3)
- Chart paper or construction paper (at least 18"-by-24") for student representations: 1 per pair (Sessions 4 and 5)
- Clipboards: 1 per pair (Sessions 4 and 5)
- Chart paper (All sessions)
- Markers and crayons, (All sessions)

Other Preparation

For Sessions 1 and 2

- Duplicate Student Sheet 3, Teeth Data, 1 per pair.
- On chart paper prepare a master list of class names on which you will collect data.
- Prepare a list of class names for student use. The names should be in the same sequence as the master list. Make several copies of the class list for each student.

For Session 3

- Duplicate Student Sheet 4, Planning a Data Collection Project, 1 per student.
- On chart paper, prepare six grade level posters, labeled *Preschool, Kindergarten, Grade 1, Grade 3, Grade 4, Grade 5 and Older*, for organizing homework data. On each poster, form two columns labeled *Name* and *Number of Teeth Lost*, so that students can list their data.
- Make arrangements with teachers from other classrooms (grades K–4) for pairs of students to come in and collect data from their students at the beginning of Session 4. Get a class list of names from each classroom.
- Prepare index cards for each K–4 classroom that students will collect data from. On each card write the teacher's name, the grade, and the room number.
- Gather materials for data collection such as clipboards, interlocking cubes, stick-on notes, markers, and so on.

For Sessions 4 and 5

- Duplicate Student Sheet 5, Looking at Data, 1 per student.

For Session 6

- Duplicate Student Sheets 6–9, Mystery Teeth Data, 1 sheet per student.
- Duplicate Student Sheets 10 and 11, Which Class Is It?, 1 of each per student.
- Label four sheets of chart paper, one label per sheet *Classroom A, Classroom B, Classroom C*, and *Classroom D*.

How Many Teeth Have You Lost?

Materials

- *How Many Teeth?* by Paul Showers (or another book about teeth, optional)
- Interlocking cubes (class set)
- Class list of names (1 per student)
- Master list of class names
- Stick-on notes (1 per student)
- Large paper (1 per pair)
- Student Sheet 3 (1 per pair)
- Chart paper

What Happens

Students collect data that represent the number of teeth they have lost. They build a cube tower representation and make a line plot with stick-on notes, then compare these two representations of the data. Pairs of students create their own representations of the teeth data. At the end of Session 2, a class discussion focuses on different representations of the same data set. For homework, students collect data about the number of teeth lost by their siblings. This data will be used in Session 3. Their work focuses on:

- collecting data
- representing data with cube towers and stick-on notes
- representing data in different ways

Start-Up

Today's Number

Calendar Date *and* Number of School Days Students express Today's Number using pennies, nickels, dimes, and quarters. For example, if Today's Number is 27 (calendar date), possible combinations are: 25¢ + 2¢ or 10¢ + 10¢ + 5¢ + 1¢ +1¢. If Today's Number is over 100, such as 127, a possible combination is: 25¢ + 25¢ + 25¢ + 25¢ + 25¢ + 1¢ + 1¢. If you are keeping track of the number of school days, add a card to the class counting strip and fill in another number on the blank 200 chart. Pose some of the following questions:

- **How many more days until we have been in school (30/130) days? How can you tell?**
- **How many more days until we have been in school (40/140) days?**
- **Which block will I fill in when we have been in school (35/135) days? How can you tell?**

Teeth Towers

Introduce this data collection activity by reading *How Many Teeth?* by Paul Showers. If you do not have this book, substitute another fiction or nonfiction book about teeth or losing teeth.

After reading the book to students, ask them about their own experiences with losing teeth. Students often remember all the details surrounding the event of loosing a tooth. You may want to ask a few students to share these stories. This might be a sensitive subject for some second grade students, especially if they have not yet lost a tooth. The **Teacher Note**, Dealing with Sensitive Issues: But I Haven't Lost a Tooth Yet (p. 52), offers suggestions for dealing with these issues in the classroom.

We are going to investigate the number of teeth lost by students in our class. First we'll collect the data as a whole class, and then you will work with partners to organize the data in some way.

Organize students into pairs. Each pair will need interlocking cubes and a class list of names. Students can use the class list to keep track of the number of teeth lost by each student. They will need this information later in the session.

First, students build a cube tower to represent the total number of teeth they have lost. As they are doing this, distribute stick-on notes and have students write on the note the number of teeth they have lost. This note is then attached to the cube tower. Students who have not yet lost any teeth will not have a tooth tower, but they should make a stick-on note that shows their data.

Display a master class list that you have prepared on chart paper or on the chalkboard. Beginning at the top of the list, call on one student at a time to put his or her tower in the middle of a circle on the floor or on the chalkboard ledge.

Angel, how many teeth have you lost? Please put your tower (with its stick-on note) here in the middle of the rug. Everyone should write 4 next to Angel's name. OK, Ayaz, you're next. How many teeth have you lost?

As each student contributes his or her data, the others record that information on their class lists as you record it on your list. At this point, do not group and organize the teeth towers unless students do so as they contribute their towers.

Making a Line Plot

Last week when we collected pocket data we talked about different ways to organize the cube towers. Now let's think about how we might organize these stick-on notes as a way of showing the information.

Students should be seated in a circle around their cube towers. Place a large sheet of chart paper next to the cube towers. Take a few of the stick-on notes off of the towers and begin to organize them into a line plot on the paper. You might begin by stacking two 1's, then a few 3's and 4's. Leave a space for the 2's, explaining why as you move the stick-on notes.

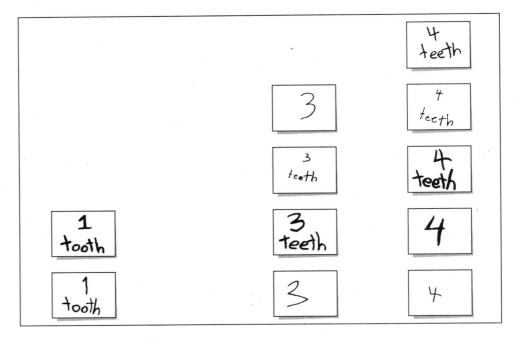

Invite students to add stick-on notes to the line plot. When all the notes have been transferred, discuss the data.

What do you notice about the shape of these data? How does it look to you?

Depending on the data set and how they have chosen to organize it, students will describe the data in different ways. Describing the shape of the data is one way of looking at the data as a whole set instead of at specific data points. It also gives students a visual image of the data and gets them to focus on important attributes of the data instead of on specific points. For example, "It's least to most," "It is like stairs," "It's all bunched together at 3 and 4."

Looking at this new graph, what can you say about the number of teeth lost by students in our classroom?

Students are likely to focus in on how many people have lost different numbers of teeth. As they do this, refer to the teeth towers and find those same data.

Chen noticed that five people have lost 4 teeth. Let's check the teeth towers. How many towers of 4 cubes do you think there should be?

Invite one student to come up and find the towers that represent 4 teeth. Group those together to verify the response.

The cube towers and the line plot made from stick-on notes are two different types of representations of the same data set. The towers represent each individual tooth within each piece of data, while each stick-on note represents a set of teeth (one note may represent 4 teeth). The **Teacher Note**, Different Representations of the Same Data (p. 53), offers information and examples about each representation.

For each observation that a student makes about the line plot (stick-on notes), ask if he or she can see that same information in the cube tower representation. Some information may be easier to see than others. For example, if the towers have not been grouped and ordered, it may be difficult to see the range (least to most) in the teeth towers but quite easy to see the range in the line plot representation.

Some information will be represented on the line plot but not in the teeth towers. For example, zero teeth will be recorded on the stick-on notes but probably not shown with the cubes. You might ask all the people who have lost zero teeth to stand up or raise their hands so that they can be compared with the number of stick-on notes.

In this brief discussion, it is most important for students to recognize the "many-to-one" relationship of the cube towers to stick-on notes. That is, each stick-on note represents a different tower. A tower and a note both represent the number of teeth lost by one child. A longer discussion comparing representations takes place at the end of Session 2.

Making a Representation

Using the data that they have collected on their class list, pairs of students create their own representations of the teeth data.

You and your partner are going to make your own representation of our class's teeth data. First you and your partner will have to agree on how to show the teeth data and how to organize them so that they show the number of teeth lost by each student in our class. Next you need to decide what materials you would like to use. Your final representation should show the number of teeth lost by each student in our class.

Remind students of some of the ways they organized and represented data in the previous investigations (people graph, the line plot, the name graph, the pocket towers, and the stick-on note graph). Depending on how familiar students are with creating data representations, brainstorm together ways they might display the data, how they could use the class list to keep track of the data, and what types of materials they might use. Interlocking cubes, tiles, counters, stick-on notes, and pencil and paper are all possible materials.

Each pair of students will need to draw a picture of their representation. If students decide to represent the data using color tiles, explain that they will then transfer that representation onto paper so that they can keep a record of their work. Distribute a large piece of paper on which students can record their representations.

Observing the Students

For the remainder of Session 1 and part of Session 2, partners organize and represent the teeth data. As students are working, use the following questions to guide your observations:

- How are students keeping track of the data? Are they using the class list? Do they check to see if everyone's data are represented? Do they check to see if the pieces of data on their graph correspond to the number of people who contributed information?
- How have students chosen to represent the data? Do they show each individual tooth in a way similar to the teeth towers, or do they use one cube or square to represent one person's data? How do they represent the people who have lost zero teeth?
- Do they group and/or order their data? If so, how?
- Can you tell by looking at their representation what it is about?

If a representation is unclear, you might ask one of the following questions to gain further insight into students' thinking and possibly help them clarify their ideas for displaying the data.

- **Can you tell me about how you are showing our teeth data?**
- **How did you show the number of teeth lost by each student?**
- **How many teeth did you lose? Did anyone else lose the same number of teeth as you did? Can you show me all the people who lost [4] teeth?**

Students' explanations can give you an indication of whether their chosen way to represent the data makes sense to them. There will be representations that do not make sense to you or do not fully communicate the story of the data gathered. Organizing and representing data develops as students try it and observe what others do. Allow representations to stand. As students share their representations, they often notice inaccuracies in them and make the necessary adjustments.

Does the Representation Tell a Story?

Some students will need to finish their representations during Session 2. As students finish their representations, they can join another pair to look at and discuss each other's work. When everyone is finished, introduce Student Sheet 3, Teeth Data.

One of the important things about making a representation is that it communicates information to others. In a way it tells the story of the data that have been collected. When you and your partner have finished organizing your data, look at the questions on Student Sheet 3 and see if you can answer them by looking at your representation.

As students finish their representations, ask them to complete the student sheet about their own graph. Students should be able to answer the questions by looking at how they organized their information. These sheets can be kept with their representations or in their math folders.

❖ **Tip for the Linguistically Diverse Classroom** Read each question on Student Sheet 3 aloud. As you do so, draw rebuses on the board to represent the question, or point to examples. To answer question 2, suggest that students draw a picture of their representation on the back of the paper. To answer question 8, suggest that students circle any part of the data that they think is unusual.

Preparing for the Discussion As students are working on their representations and Student Sheet 3, walk around and pick two or three representations to use to focus the upcoming discussion on Different Ways to Represent the Same Data. Choose representations that show:

- different ways of using the same materials
- the names of students and how many teeth they lost vs. the number of people who have lost a certain number of teeth
- instances where you can clearly see least/most and instances where you can't

If students do not complete this sheet, they may finish it another time so they can participate in the class discussion. You may wish to use the list of questions on page 49, as you review students' responses to Student Sheet 3.

Class Discussion: Different Ways to Represent the Same Data

Leave 15 minutes at the end of Session 2 for this discussion. Gather students together so they can see the representations of the teeth data. The **Dialogue Box**, Representing Teeth Data (p. 54), is an example of how one teacher facilitated the sharing of representations in the classroom.

Begin by asking one pair of students to share their representation with the class. Let them explain how they organized their data, then ask the rest of the class to think about their own representations.

Think about the way you organized the teeth data. Was it like this way?

Some students might say that they used the same materials but organized them in a different way. For example, one pair of students might have built 30 cube towers representing the number of teeth lost by each student in the class. Another pair might also have used cubes but organized them into a line plot of sorts, with each cube representing one person and a certain number of teeth.

Your questions for this discussion will depend in part on the types of representations you have chosen. Important ideas to bring out are that the same information can be represented in different ways and that sometimes you can see different things about the data depending on how you have chosen to organize it.

Let's take a look at Trini and Rosie's graph. On their graph you can see how many teeth each person lost and who those people are. Who else has a representation that shows who lost what amount of teeth? Who has a representation where you can't tell individual people but you can tell how many teeth each person lost?

At the end of the discussion, pose the following question:

If we visited another second grade class, what do you think their data would look like? The same as ours? Different from ours? Why? Share your ideas with your partner.

After discussion between partners, ask students to share their ideas with the class. Record these ideas on chart paper and save this for list for Session 3.

Weekly Logs This is a good time for students to record the work that they have done in making representations in their Weekly Logs. Encourage them to record problems they are having and the solution methods that they found. Work individually with students to review their logs.

Sessions 1 and 2 Follow-Up

- Students collect teeth data from siblings. They record the name, grade, and number of teeth lost for each sibling. An only child may ask a friend, cousin, or neighbor. They will need these data for the first activity of Session 3.

- Students also count the number of teeth they currently have. This information could be organized into another representation, called How Many Teeth Do You Have?

How Many Teeth Has Our Class Lost? Give each student or pairs of students a set of the teeth data from your classroom and ask them to calculate the total number of teeth lost.

Dealing with Sensitive Issues: But I Haven't Lost a Tooth Yet

Students get most engaged in projects that deal with real data and real-life situations. But these compelling topics can also touch on sensitive subjects. You can anticipate some topics that might be emotional for some students. For example, when collecting data on the number of people in a family or the number of siblings, you might be aware of family situations such as divorce, remarriage, or even death. Other situations, such as losing teeth, can catch you totally by surprise as having a powerful impact on some students.

This is not to say that we should avoid these issues but rather that we should consider how topics are introduced to students. In the teeth example, acknowledging (prior to collecting data) that not all second grade students have lost a tooth or that some younger students may have lost more teeth allows students who fall into these categories to share that information (if they want). It also makes other students aware that all of their classmates may not share the same experience or data as they do.

Losing a first tooth is an important event in many children's lives. It is a physical milestone as well as an emotional/social milestone. It is important to reassure those students who have not lost a tooth or who have lost many teeth that people grow and develop at different rates and that losing teeth is one of the things that happen to people in different ways and on different schedules. Often it is helpful to broaden this discussion by thinking about other sorts of milestones or important events in students' lives that happen in different ways and at different times. Learning to read, growing taller, and riding a two-wheeler are all familiar and important to most seven- and eight-year-olds. By acknowledging these differences you can help to create a climate of acceptance and awareness in your classroom.

Different Representations of the Same Data

Organizing the same data in more than one way can often make certain features of the data more visible or prominent. Consider the following representations of the same set of teeth data.

The representation below shows the teeth data using towers of interlocking cubes—one tower represents one student's data, and within each tower you can see each individual tooth. For every tooth lost there is a cube.

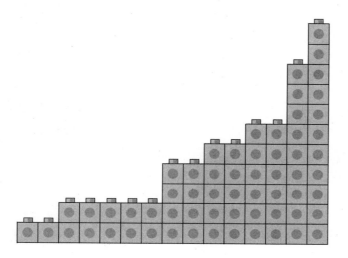

Below is a line plot made with stick-on notes. Each note stands for one person's data. Where it is placed on the line tells how many teeth were lost.

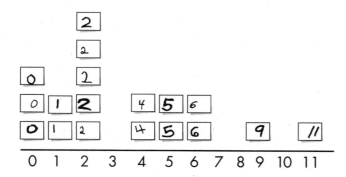

In both representations it is possible to see many of the same features, but there are also differences. For example, with the cube towers it is difficult to represent zero teeth, thus making the range appear to be between 1 and 11 rather than 0 and 11. On the line plot it may be easier for some students to see that more people had lost 2 teeth than any other number, and it is easier to identify places where there are no data (3, 7, 8, 10).

The tooth tower representation allows students to see almost every piece of information. (It does not, however, allow students to see how many children have not lost teeth.) Calculating the total number of teeth or determining how many teeth if two people each had lost five teeth is an easier task for many second grade students using the cube tower representations. The cubes make it possible to count each tooth, whereas in order to figure out this information using the line plot, students must be able to translate each note into the correct number of teeth. They must be able to work with groups and understand the idea of many-to-one.

Often line plots are the predominant type of graph that young students are introduced to, and although they are an important type of representation, many students (especially students younger than second grade) are not yet able to interpret the information represented. They may be able to tell you that there are two squares or stick-on notes at 6, but many confuse whether this information represents teeth or people, and few understand that those two notes really represent 12 teeth.

It is important for students to see data represented in both ways and to try to make connections between the two types of representations. Questions such as, "Chen noticed that five people have each lost two teeth. Can you find that information on our stick-on note?" help students see that the same data can be represented in different ways.

━ D I A L O G U E ☐ B O X ━

Representing Teeth Data

This discussion takes place during the activity Different Ways to Represent the Same Data (p. 50), and focuses on sharing different ways to organize and represent data. Students have just finished working with the class set of teeth data. The teacher has decided to highlight a few different ways of keeping track of the data. By asking students questions about their representations, the teacher acknowledges that different representations of the same data set allow you to see different types of information.

Ping and Laura made a representation that is similar to the line plot we made when we collected data about the number of siblings we have. Can you explain how you kept track of all your data?

Ping: Well, we checked names off on a class list.

Laura: First we put the numbers in order along this bottom part, then when Ping told me a person's name and how many teeth they lost, I made an X on that number.

Ping: And I checked off the name.

Think about whether you kept track of your data in a way that was similar to or different from Ping and Laura's.

Phoebe: We wrote the numbers of how many teeth people had lost along the bottom and then we took turns counting numbers for each number of teeth. So on my turn I counted up the number of people who had lost 1 tooth and that was 2. So then I put two 2's on top of the 2 row.

Imani: We counted on the class list.

Tory: We used the class list, but instead of X's we used cubes and built towers. A tower for each person.

Angel: At first Tory made all the boys' towers and I made the girls', but we got a little mixed up because it was hard to remember where you were. So then we started checking names off on the list.

Tory: And then we counted all the towers and all the names on the list and made sure it was the same number.

The class agrees that checking names off or crossing them out is a good way to keep track of the data that have been counted.

Look at your representations. Is it clear what numbers of teeth *no one* has lost?

Ayaz: On our graph we only showed the numbers where people lost teeth. [*Ayaz has made a bar graph with color tiles. The range on the bottom of his graph shows the numbers 1, 2, 4, 5, 7, 9.*]

Juanita: We made towers, and unless you organize them into groups then it's too hard to see which numbers of teeth no one has lost.

Franco: Because numbers go in order. If you don't put them in order then it's too hard to tell if something is missing.

So it seems like putting the data in order is a helpful way of seeing amounts that you have data for and amounts where there are no data. I also notice that some of you, like Phoebe and Lionel and Olga and Simon, included information about who has lost a certain number of teeth.

Simon: I wanted to make sure I knew which stick-on note was for my data, so that's why we put names on all the notes.

Sometimes it is important to know which person the data represented. When you represent your data you make different choices about what to include and what not to include. That's a choice you make. It's interesting to think about how those choices can show different pieces of information and how we can see different things by looking at different representations.

Comparing Lost Teeth Among Other Grades

What Happens

Students post the teeth data that they collected as homework. As a class they make and discuss predictions about collecting teeth data from other classes. In pairs they write and draw plans and organize materials so that they can collect data the following day. Their work focuses on:

■ making predictions about data based on a small sample
■ planning and organizing a data collection project

Start-Up

Today's Number

Calendar Date *and* Number of School Days Suggest that students use doubles as you work together brainstorming ways to express Today's Number. For example, if Today's Number is 28 (calendar date), some possible expressions are: 14 + 14; 7 + 7 + 7 + 7; and 10 + 10 + 4 + 4. If students are working with a larger number, such as 149, some possible expressions are: 50 + 50 + 20 + 20 + 4 + 4 + 1 and 75 + 75 − 1. Add a card to the class counting strip and fill in another number on the blank 200 chart if you are keeping track of the number of days in school.

How Many Teeth Do You Have? Ask students to share their methods from the homework for how they counted their teeth. If you plan to use these data, arrange for a place where students can post them.

Materials

■ Prepared grade-level posters (6 sheets)
■ Prepared index cards (about 20)
■ Class list of names from other classrooms
■ Materials for data collection
■ Student Sheet 4 (1 per student)

Activity

Looking at Sibling Teeth Data

As students arrive in the classroom, they write their homework data on the prepared grade-level posters. One way to organize the data is to list two columns on each poster labeled *Name* and *Number of Teeth Lost.*

For the last two math classes we have been organizing data about the number of teeth lost by students in our classroom. Yesterday we discussed how our teeth data might compare to a set of data from another second grade class.

Review the list of ideas from yesterday's discussion.

Explain to students that they will be investigating the number of teeth lost by younger and older students in other classes at the school. They will collect data from other classrooms in the school, organize their data, and then represent it in some way.

Last night for homework you collected some information about the number of teeth lost by older and younger children. Let's look at the kindergarten poster. What do you notice about the data we collected about children who are in kindergarten?

Create a quick line plot based on the data at the bottom of the poster. Encourage students to look carefully at the data that have been collected and describe what they see. Students may notice that no one lost more than 4 teeth or that 3 kids lost 2 teeth.

Do these data match your experience?

Students may share stories about themselves, friends, or relatives who are not listed on the data set. For example, "Some kindergartners could lose no teeth, because I know someone who hasn't lost any yet," or "My cousin is in first grade and she's only lost 4 teeth, but when I was in first grade I lost 7."

Soon we will be going to collect data from students in other classrooms. When you go to a classroom of kindergarten students, what kind of data do you think you will get? What numbers of teeth are likely to appear?

Although this may only be a small sample of data, students might be able to make some predictions from it, such as, "I don't think anybody will have lost 8 teeth, that's too many," or "I think for third grade there will be a lot of numbers in the teens, because I know someone in third grade who lost 14 teeth." Help students extend their thinking by asking them to describe the range of teeth lost and the mode.

We found that kids in our class had lost between 0 and 10 teeth. What might the range be in the kindergarten class we visit? Why?

In our classroom most kids have lost 8 teeth [*insert the mode or most typical for your class*]. **What do you think will be the most common number of teeth lost in a kindergarten classroom? Why?**

Record students' predictions for each grade level at the bottom of each poster.

For each poster, use the data students recorded to make a line plot. You can draw the line plot on the bottom of the poster. Then ask students to use this line plot to predict what they might find out when they collect data in other classrooms. Encourage students to pay attention to the range and mode of the data.

Save these predictions for students to reconsider during the discussion at the end of Session 5, after they have collected data from other classrooms.

Activity

Organize students into pairs for the project of collecting data from other classrooms. Depending on the number of students in your class and the number of classes in your school, you may need to assign two pairs to the same class. This is fine; they can compare their data and representations. Assign classrooms by distributing the index cards listing the teacher's name and classroom grade. Some teachers have found it helpful to have a "master list" posted in the classroom. This list should include the names of teachers, grade level, and students who are assigned to collect data from that classroom.

Discuss with your partner how you are going to collect data from the students in your assigned classroom. You'll need to find out how many teeth each person in the class has lost. Think about all the different ways that we have collected data. Talk about a plan with your partner and then decide what materials you will need.

Distribute Student Sheet 4, Planning a Data Collection Project, to each student. Students can use these sheets to help organize their plan.

Organizing the Teeth Data Project

Students' plans will vary. Some pairs or groups may decide to collect the data by interviewing each student and recording the number of teeth lost on a class list. Some may want to make a graph that they bring to the class and have each student respond. Still others might bring cubes and ask class members to make cube towers that correspond to the number of teeth they have lost. These cubes towers are then brought back to the classroom as "raw data," which students organize and use as a representation.

When students have a plan for collecting data from another class, they review their plan with you. Students then gather materials they will need to collect the data. Materials can be labeled and stored in a small box, bag, or envelope until the next math session.

Allowing students to organize their data collection plan in a way makes sense to them is a rich experience. Students have the opportunity to generate an idea, test it, and organize the experience for themselves. This takes time, and you may need to add an extra session to the teeth project.

❖ **Tip for the Linguistically Diverse Classroom** Read each question on Student Sheet 4 aloud. Assist students in recording responses representative of their fluency level. For example, students may draw pictures on the back of the sheet to respond to the questions. Students who are able can record short written responses to some or all of the questions.

Based on the needs of students, the schedule of the school day, and the flexibility of colleagues, provide students with one plan for collecting the data. For example, give each student a class list from a different classroom and have students visit that classroom. They can spend 5 minutes collecting data from the entire group, and then return to their own room to organize and represent the data. Although students have not generated the plan for how the data will be collected, they have the experience of collecting data and can then focus on organizing, representing, and interpreting them.

Prior to sending students into classrooms, discuss how they will ask their question. Consider having students role-play how they will explain to the another class what they are investigating and how they will present their question. Brainstorm with them how they might explain their question to a kindergarten child. As students finish their planning and complete Student Sheet 4, they can rehearse how they will present their question.

Some teachers spend a considerable amount of time helping students prepare to go into another classroom. Students may be excited but also nervous about this task, especially if they go into classrooms with older students. The **Dialogue Box,** Collecting Data from Other Classrooms (p. 59), is an example of a discussion that one teacher had with students.

Note: Remind your colleagues that your students will be coming to their classrooms to collect teeth data on the following day. Depending on the size of your school, you may want to enlist the help of parent volunteers to walk students to the classrooms they will visit, and back.

Collecting Data from Other Classrooms

This dialogue, which takes place as students prepare to collect data from other classrooms (p. 57) recounts their feelings of nervousness and also their enthusiasm.

Naomi: Do the teachers know we are coming?

Yes, and they are happy about it.

Salim: We are going to use the class lists to check everyone off. But what if we can't read the names on the class list?

Graham: You could ask a kid in the classroom. Or you could ask a teacher; that's what teachers are there for.

Good suggestions.

Jeffrey: What if you are sort of embarrassed? I don't think I'd be embarrassed if I was going to a first grade classroom, but I'm going to a fourth grade.

Any ideas about what to do?

Rosie: I'd try to look for someone in the class that I know.

Jeffrey: But what if you're embarrassed, and what if someone laughs?

The teacher in the classroom is there to help you collect the data. Going into a classroom of older students is not an easy thing for some people to do. Jeffrey, how about if I walk down to your classroom with you and your partner and stay around until you get started?

Karina: Well, in our group, Tim said that he doesn't talk to people he doesn't know, so we decided that he could check off the names and write down the numbers and I would ask the questions.

After students return from collecting their data (Session 4), the teacher gathers them together for a discussion before they begin organizing the data. The discussion shifts from how they were feeling about collecting the data to things that they noticed about the data they collected.

Before you left, some of you talked about how you felt about going into other classrooms. How did it go?

Carla: It was much easier than I thought it would be, but I was a little embarrassed.

Rosie: I was a tiny bit scared.

Graham: I got a little nervous because we knocked on the door twice and the teacher didn't hear us, so we just had to open the door and we couldn't say excuse me because the teacher was talking. And finally the teacher saw us.

Ebony: I thought it was exciting. Very fun!

Troy: I was kind of surprised because I was expecting that people would have high numbers because we were in a fourth grade. I was surprised that some students had lost fewer teeth than some second graders.

Jess: I thought most kids in kindergarten would have lost 2 or 3 or 4 teeth, but it wasn't that way. Lots lost 1.

Laura: I was surprised that in fourth grade only one person lost 6 teeth and one person said they lost 16. That surprised me because that's a *lot* of teeth.

Imani: We went to the kindergarten class, and we thought the numbers would be zero, 1, and 2—and they were!

I'm impressed by your thinking. You really thought about what might happen with the data before you collected it.

Sessions 4 and 5

Collecting Teeth Data

Materials

- Data plans from previous session (Student Sheet 4)
- Materials for data collection
- Large sheets of paper (1 per pair)
- Markers, crayons
- Student Sheet 5 (1 per student)
- Posters with student predictions from Session 3
- Clipboards (1 per pair)

What Happens

After a quick review of their data plans, pairs of students go to other classrooms to collect teeth data. They make a representation of these data using pencil and paper. They use Student Sheet 5 as a guide for making sure their representation communicates certain information. At the end of Session 5, the class discusses their findings. This project is used as an assessment for students' understanding of collecting, organizing, and representing data. Their work focuses on:

- collecting, organizing, and representing a set of numerical data
- interpreting data
- making general comparisons of data from two groups

Start-Up

Today's Number

Calendar Date *and* Number of School Days Suggest that students express Today's Number using pennies, nickels, dimes, and quarters. For example, if Today's Number is 30 (calendar date), possible combinations include: 25¢ + 5¢ or 10¢ + 10¢ + 5¢ + 5¢. If Today's Number is over 100—for example, 150—a possible combination is: 25¢ + 25¢ + 25¢ + 25¢ + 25¢ + 10¢ + 10¢ + 5¢. If you are keeping track of the number of school days, add a card to the class counting strip and fill in another number on the blank 200 chart.

Activity

Collecting Teeth Data from Other Classrooms

Students spend the first 5 to 10 minutes of this session reviewing their plans for how they will collect data in their assigned classroom. Each pair of students should have all of the materials that they gathered from the previous session. Remind students that they need to collect data from each student in their assigned classroom.

Gathering these data should not take a long time. Each teacher is expecting you. After you have collected all of your data, you and your partner should come back to our classroom and start making plans for how you will organize and represent the data.

Show students the large sheets of paper, clipboards, markers, and crayons that they can use to make their representation. Each pair of students should make a representation that can be posted and saved. Then, as students are ready, send pairs or groups off to collect their data.

Note: When students return from their assigned classrooms, they may be excited and eager to share their experiences. You may want to plan 5–10 minutes as a sharing time and as a time to refocus for the next step of this data project.

Activity

Teacher Checkpoint

Organizing and Representing Teeth Data

Students spend the remainder of this session and about half of the next session organizing the teeth data they collected. Students will need a large flat surface to work on.

You need to decide how to organize the data you collected and how to record the data on paper. Just like we did with our own teeth data and with the pocket data, decide on a way of arranging your data so that someone could look at it and tell what your representation is about and how many teeth were lost by students in the classroom you visited.

Distribute Student Sheet 5 to students. Tell them that when they have finished with their representations, they should answer the questions on this student sheet.

❖ **Tip for the Linguistically Diverse Classroom** Read each question on Student Sheet 5 aloud. Students can relate what they did through pictures and a few words. For example, students can respond with one word or one numeral for questions 1, 3, and 4. They can draw a picture of their representation for question 5 and draw a ring around what they thought was interesting for question 6. Suggest that students put an exclamation mark on their picture over anything that surprised them to respond to question 7.

Observing the Students

Since this activity engages students in all aspects of data analysis, it can be used as an opportunity to assess students' understanding of gathering, organizing, representing, and interpreting data. In assessing students' understanding, consider the data plans and representations they generate, as well as your observations of them as they are working and the conversations you have with them about their work. If you have taught other *Investigations* units, you will be familiar with some different ways of recording and keeping track of your observations of students. The **Teacher Note**, Keeping Track of Students' Work (p. 64), offers some suggestions for documenting your observations.

As students are working, try to get a sense of the following:

- How are students organizing their data?
- Do they have a system for keeping track of the data they collected?
- What sort of representations do they make? Do they communicate information in a way that is understandable to them? to others? Are they able to transfer the data from their original recording sheet so that they represent all of it?
- If students are using a line plot, do they have a baseline that indicates the numbers of teeth? Does it go up by 1, leaving space for data that they did not have, or do they label only those amounts of lost teeth for which they actually have data? What did they do about zero?

Students will vary in their abilities to make a representation that communicates all of these things. If you notice something that is unclear about a representation, you might ask the student to explain his or her reasoning. If something is missing, you might say, "I noticed that three people in this class lost four teeth. Can you show me where that information is?" Students will correct or adapt that which makes sense to them. Don't insist that every graph be perfect. Students' understanding of organizing and representing data develops over time.

As students finish, encourage them to look at each other's representations. About 20 minutes before the end of class, gather students together for a discussion about their representations.

Activity

Class Discussion: Comparing the Data

Ask students to describe how they collected their data in other classrooms. As a method is described, ask students if they used that same method. Then ask those who used a different method to describe what they did. In this way you acknowledge all students without having every pair share its method.

Ask all students who collected information from a kindergarten classroom to stand up in front of the group with their representations. While one student holds the representation, the partner should briefly explain what they learned about the group of students they collected data from. If you have more than one representation from the same grade level, ask students to compare what's the same and what's different about each representation.

For each grade level you might also ask students to compare the data and to see if or how they vary from class to class. Some easy comparisons to make are:

- the range of data from each class
- the most common number of teeth lost by students in that class

■ any unusual pieces of data. (One kindergartner had lost nine teeth. This was an unusual piece of data that the second graders insisted on double-checking.)

Record students' observations on chart paper so that these can be posted along with the representations.

After students have shared their findings, return to some of the predictions that were made in Session 3 about the number of teeth lost by older and younger students.

A few days ago when we made predictions about how our class's data would compare to the teeth data from a younger class, someone thought that first graders would have lost teeth fewer teeth than second graders. Based on the data we collected, is that true? Can you look at the representations from the first grade and determine whether that is true?

Here's another prediction: Older students will have lost more teeth than younger students. Look at the representations and see if there is a way of determining whether this is true.

If you do not have time to discuss all of the representations or predictions, you can return to them at other times during the day and over the next few days. Post student representations and perhaps their predictions and their observations. You might consider posting these in the hallway of your school so that they can be viewed by other classes or students.

The discussion of data and this data collection project may generate related questions about teeth. Some students might be interested in investigating one of these questions as part of their self-selected data project in the next investigation.

The **Teacher Note,** Looking at Teeth Graphs (p. 65), gives some examples of student representations and highlights some aspects of student-generated graphs in second grade.

Sessions 4 and 5 Follow-Up

■ **Displaying the Teeth Data** Invite other classes in to see the graphs of their class. Have second graders explain the project and their findings.

■ **Total Number of Teeth Lost** Students calculate the total number of teeth lost in the class they collected data from. Post this information for each classroom. Some students might calculate the total number of teeth lost by the third grade, whereas others might want to calculate the total number of teeth lost by all of the classrooms surveyed.

 **Extensions**

Throughout the *Investigations* curriculum there are numerous opportunities to observe students as they work. Teacher observations are an important part of ongoing assessment. Individual observations are snapshots of a student's experience with a single activity. When considered over time, a set of observations can provide an informative and detailed picture. These observations can be useful in documenting and assessing a student's growth. They offer important information when preparing for family conferences or writing student reports.

Your observations of students will vary throughout the year. At times you may be interested in particular strategies that students are developing to solve problems. Or you might want to observe how students use or do not use materials to help them solve problems. At other times you may be interested in noting the strategy that a student uses when playing a game during Choice Time. Class discussions also provide many opportunities to take note of students' ideas and thinking.

Keeping observation notes on a class of 28 students can become overwhelming and time-consuming. You will probably find it necessary to develop some sort of system to make recording and keeping track of your observations of students. While a few ideas and suggestions are offered here, the most important aspect of developing a tracking system is finding one that works for you.

A class list of names is a convenient way of jotting down observations of students. Since the space is limited, it is not possible to write lengthy notes. However, when kept over time, these short observations provide important information.

Stick-on address labels can be kept on clipboards around the room. Notes can be taken on individual students and then these labels can be peeled off and stuck into a file that you set up for each student.

Alternatively, you might find that jotting down brief notes at the end of each week works well for you. Some teachers find that this is a useful way of reflecting on the class as a whole, on the curriculum, and on individual students. Planning for the next weeks' activities often develops from these weekly reflections.

In addition to your keeping notes on students, each student will keep a folder of work. This work and the daily entries on the Weekly Logs can document a student's experience. Together they can help you keep track of the students in your classroom, assess their growth over time, and communicate this information to others. At the end of each unit there is a list of things you might choose to keep in students' folders.

Looking at Teeth Graphs

Included here are examples of student-generated representations of the teeth data that they collected. In this class, most students chose to represent the data using a bar graph or line plot. While these representations are similar in some ways, it is interesting to note how each group documented the range of data and how different groups chose to represent zero. Often when students are made aware of this dilemma, they feel that it is important to hold a place for zero or make some sort of mark that indicates zero. This is the case with three of the graphs. Only in the

first graph did students acknowledge zero within the range of possible numbers of teeth. Here the students showed that one person lost zero teeth and that no one lost 1, 7, 9, or 10 teeth.

Interestingly, students had a far easier time representing "zero people" in a particular category. In Graph 1 students left blank spaces to indicate that no people had lost that number of teeth. The other graphs show zero people in a category by using a special symbol or simply by labeling that category "0".

Graph 1

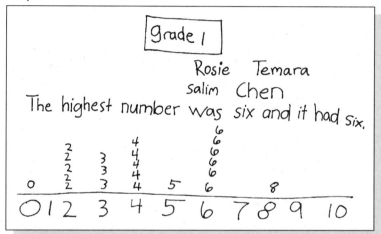

Graph 2

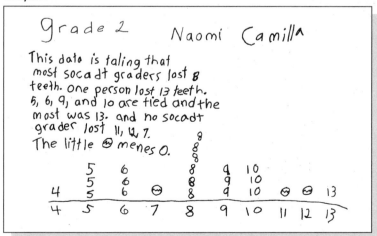

Continued on next page

Students' interpretations of their data varied considerably. Graphs 1 and 2 describe some feature of the data—how many people lost a certain number of teeth. Graphs 3 and 4 offer a bit more analysis. In Graph 4, students notice that there is a clump of data between 5 and 8. This is significant in that they are able to comment that "Most people lost between 5 and 8 teeth," thus making a generalization about the number of teeth lost in that second grade classroom. The analysis of data in Graph 3 begins to compare the fourth grade data to their second grade data. They notice that although in both grades 8 teeth was the number most kids lost, they begin to look at how the data were distributed—noting that more people lost higher numbers of teeth in fourth grade than in second grade.

Graph 3

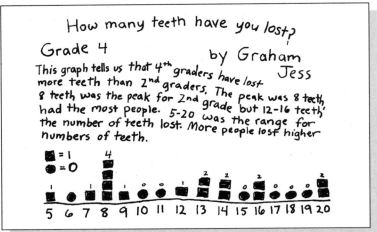

Graph 4

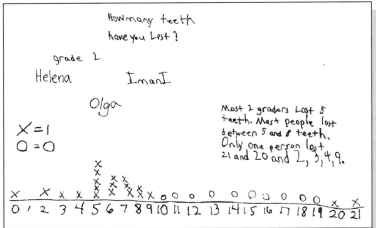

Mystery Teeth Data

What Happens

Students consider sets of Mystery Teeth Data collected from different grade levels. They create a pencil-and-paper representation of one set of data and exchange representations. Students then determine which set of Mystery Teeth Data their representation portrays. As a class they make hypotheses about which grade level (K–4) the representations could represent based on the data, the representation, and their previous work with collecting teeth data from other classrooms. Their work focuses on:

- creating a representation from a set of data
- looking at important features of a data set
- making a hypothesis based on a set of data and a representation

Start-Up

Today's Number

- **Calendar Date** If you are using the calendar date for Today's Number, work with students to brainstorm ways of expressing the number using combinations of 10. For example, if the number they are working on is 25 and one number sentence is 10 +10 + 5, ask students if there is another way of making 10, such as (6 + 4) + (6 + 4) + 5 or (4 + 3 + 2 + 1) + (4 + 3 + 2 + 1) + 5. Record their expressions on chart paper.

- **Number of School Days** If you are using the number of school days for Today's Number, and the number is over 100, work with students to brainstorm ways to express the number using both addition and subtraction. For example, if the number is 152, two possible solutions are: 200 – 100 + 52 and 160 – 10 + 2. Add a card to the class counting strip and fill in another number on the blank 200 chart.

Materials

- Large paper (1 per pair)
- Student Sheets 6–9 (1 sheet per student)
- Student Sheets 10 and 11 (1 per student)
- Prepared chart paper labeled *Class A* through *Class D*

Activity

Distribute one page of Mystery Teeth Data (one of Student Sheets 6, 7, 8, or 9) to each student. The four pages should be as close to equally distributed as possible. Explain that these are the data that have been collected from four different classes and that each student should make a representation of his or her data on paper. The **Teacher Note**, Mystery Teeth Data (p. 71), tells about which grade levels these data represent.

Mystery Teeth Data

Today we are going to play a matching game with some teeth data from other schools. Each of you will have one set of data to work with. You will make a representation of the data on paper. Then I'll collect your representations, mix them up, and pass them back to you. Your job then is to match the representation you have with a set of mystery data. Then, using what you know about the number of teeth lost by students of different ages, think about which grade your data could represent.

Use about half of this session for making representations and the other half for matching. If students need help getting started, remind them about the data they just collected and represented from other classrooms in your school. Explain that in this activity the data have already been collected. Have them refer to the representations they made with other data sets as possible ideas for where to start.

As students are working on their Mystery Teeth data representations, look for ways their representations have changed since the beginning of the unit. Remind students to put their names on their work, but not the letter of the class they are representing. You may want to have students record the letter of the Mystery Data they represent on paper and put it in their math folder.

If some students finish early, they can choose another set of data to represent.

Which Class
Is It?

Before collecting students' representations, post prepared chart paper labeled *Class A* through *Class D* in four different areas of the room and attach the corresponding set of the Mystery Teeth Data to each chart. Students will post their representations on the chart paper.

When students have finished their representations, collect them, mix them up, and redistribute them. Also give each student copies of Student Sheets 10 and 11, Which Class Is It?

Look at the representation you have and see if you can match it to one of the sets of Mystery Teeth Data posted on the wall. When you think you know which data set your graph represents, put your representation on the right chart, then answer the questions on Student Sheet 11.

When you made your representations, you tried to be accurate, but you might find something on your representation that does not match. If that happens, think about how to change it so it matches.

Give students 5–10 minutes to walk around the room and determine which data set they have. (Or have them use the data sets as shown on Student Sheet 10.) After they have matched and posted their representations, remind them to complete Student Sheet 11.

Some students may not accurately represent the data. The emphasis is not on getting all the information correct, but on, "Does this representation tell a story and does it tell the story that I want it to tell?" If students discover a problem with their representation, ask them how they might correct it.

❖ **Tip for the Linguistically Diverse Classroom** Ask students with a limited English proficiency to point to or ring key data that helped convince them which set of Mystery Data best matched their representation. To record a response, students can use numbers and rebuses to support their opinion. For example, students may draw 6 stick figures next to the picture of one tooth to represent 6 children losing one tooth. Then ask students to decide what grade level they think their data represents and record the number. You might ask them to explain verbally how they reached their conclusion.

Gather students together in front of the first set of Mystery Teeth Data and the posted representations.

Let's look at the representations for Class A. If you think the graph you posted represented the data from this class, could you explain why? Were there certain things about the graph that made you think it belonged to this set of data?

The **Dialogue Box**, Discussing Mystery Data (p. 72), gives some examples of student reasoning in this activity. As students offer explanations for each class, listen for some of the following ideas:

■ Do they use key pieces of data, such as five people lost four teeth or zero people lost three teeth?

■ Do they consider the range of the graph and try to match it to the range of a particular data set?

■ What aspects of the graph did they pay particular attention to as they made their decision?

■ Did they work from the information on the graph or did they work from the data sets?

■ Did anyone make a representation that is posted here but does not belong here?

The student who drew the graph and the student who placed it incorrectly talk about their decisions. Follow this procedure for each set of Mystery Data.

Depending on how the discussion proceeds, you may want to have students make some hypotheses based on the data and the representations about what grade each class represents as they discuss each set of data. Or you might discuss all the sets of Mystery Teeth Data and then end the discussion with students offering their ideas and hypotheses about which data represent which grade level.

Listen for whether students use some of the data that they just collected from their classrooms to determine what grade the Mystery Teeth Data might be from.

If you complete the discussion during this session, you will want to reveal which grade level each data set represents. By this time each student's representation should be matched correctly. When the activity has ended, students can remove their representations from the class charts, attach their set of Mystery Teeth Data (Student Sheet 6, 7, 8, or 9) to their representation, and put these sheets along with Student Sheet 11 in their math folders.

Session 6 Follow-Up

 **Extension**

Making a Data Display Consider displaying Student Sheets 6–10 and some of students' representations on a bulletin board in the hallway and posing the question: "Can you match the graph to the correct set of data?"

Mystery Teeth Data

The teeth data provided on Student Sheets 6–10 were collected from elementary classrooms in California and Massachusetts. Your students may be interested in finding out what grade each data set represents. It is suggested that you hold off sharing this information until the class has had time to consider all of the representations, look carefully at the data sets, and discuss their thinking. Quite likely you will find that given their prior experiences with collecting and considering data from their own classroom, their siblings, and older and younger students in the school, students will have some well-formed ideas about how many teeth students in different grades have lost. The **Dialogue Box**, Discussing Mystery Data (p. 72), provides some examples of student reasoning in this activity.

When students have shared their thinking and the grades have been revealed, you might want to extend the discussion by asking students if there is anything surprising about the data for each grade. They might also enjoy comparing the data they collected to these other classes.

MYSTERY TEETH DATA

Class A: 3rd grade (Cambridge, Massachusetts)

Class B: 2nd grade (Piedmont, California)

Class C: kindergarten (Goleta, California)

Class D: 4th grade (Cambridge, Massachusetts)

Discussing Mystery Data

In this discussion, related to the activity Which Class Is It? (p. 68), students have posted their representations on one of the Class Charts (A, B, C, or D), and the teacher has focused their attention on the representations for Class A.

If you think you had a graph that represented the data from Class A, can you share your thinking about how you made that decision?

Tim: First I checked to see if there was a 14 on the graph, and then I kept going down the list.

What do you mean when you say you went down the list?

Tim: Well, I looked at each list on the charts and then I saw that my graph had one 14 and two 11's, so I found the classroom that had one 14 and two 11's and I checked all the numbers.

So you tried to match a piece of data on your graph to one of the lists.

Tim: Yup.

Temara: I noticed that my graph had lots of people who had lost 8 teeth, so I looked for that clue.

Linda: On my graph there weren't any small numbers, so I knew it couldn't be Class B or C.

It's interesting that you all used a similar strategy—you looked for something important about the representation you had, like there were lots of 8's or there was only one 14, and then you used that information when you looked at all of the sets of Mystery Teeth Data.

How about Class B?

Salim: Mine was easy because of the way the graph was made. The person made a list of all the numbers of teeth and the numbers of people who lost that many. So I could see that one person lost 1 tooth, two people lost 3 teeth, and no one lost 2 teeth. And the numbers went from 1 tooth to 13 teeth, so I just looked for a set of data that had 1 to 13 teeth, and that was B.

Helena: I looked at the range on my graph, and it was easy because there weren't a lot of different numbers, and the numbers didn't go up very high.

Can you explain what you mean by that?

Helena: Well, it's only from zero teeth to 4 teeth. No one lost more than 4 teeth. And I think I know which grade Class C is from.

How many people think they know the grade of Class C? Turn to someone sitting nearby and tell him or her what you think and why you think that. [*Most students think that the data are from a kindergarten class because of the small range.*]

Tim: It's kindergarten because the numbers are really small and it practically matches the data that we collected from our kindergarten rooms. Because in the first grade lots of kids have lost 3, 4, or 5 teeth, and some have lost more, so I don't think it's a first grade.

Helena: I agree.

As you were explaining your thinking to a partner, I heard lots of you talking about the small range of numbers and also comparing the data to the data we collected. The range of numbers on a graph is one important piece of information when you are looking at data.

Jeffrey: You know what was a little confusing? I had a range of 5 teeth to 14 teeth, but then I noticed that two of the classes had that range: Classes A and D. So I couldn't just use the range.

So what other information did you use?

Jeffrey: Well, both were close, but then Paul showed me that Class D didn't have very many kids in it. So I counted the kids on my graph and there was 1 less than the number of kids on D, so I think the person forgot to put someone's teeth on the graph. But I still think it's D.

Continued on next page

I noticed that a few people commented that their graphs had some mistakes on them. Can you politely point out the differences you noticed between the graph and the set of data to the author?

In this discussion, students used a variety of strategies to match representations to the Mystery Teeth Data that they represented. Some students looked for important features of the data such as the most common number of teeth lost ("there were lots of 8's"), while others considered the range of the graph and the range of the data sets. In this class, most students seemed to work from the information on the graph to the data sets. Noticing important features of a graph is an important part of analyzing data.

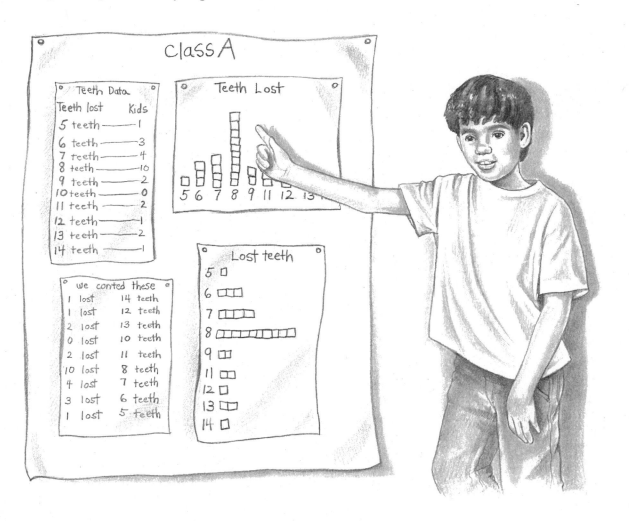

Data Projects

What Happens

Session 1: Choosing a Question to Investigate
As a class, students brainstorm a list of possible things they could collect data about. In pairs they choose a question to investigate and begin to plan their data analysis project.

Sessions 2, 3, and 4: Collecting, Organizing, and Representing Data Students collect, organize, and represent the data they have collected. They write a summary describing and interpreting these data.

Session 5: Data Projects: What Does This Graph Tell Us? Data representations are displayed in the classroom and viewed by students, families, or other invited classes. Students explain their representations to visitors and answer questions about their data project.

Mathematical Emphasis

- Planning a data analysis project
- Engaging in all phases of data analysis, including collecting, organizing, representing, and interpreting data
- Using data representations to communicate information

Questions We Might Investigate

How many movies have you seen this year?
How many times have you been on a Ferris wheel?
How many times can you hop on one foot in a minute?
How many cousins do you have?

What to Plan Ahead of Time

Materials

- Chart paper (Session 1)
- Materials for data collection (Sessions 1–4)
- Markers or crayons (Sessions 2–4)
- Large paper or chart paper: 1 per pair (Sessions 2–4)

Other Preparation

For Session 1

- Duplicate Student Sheet 4, Planning a Data Collection Project, 1 per pair.
- As in Investigation 2, provide materials for students to use during data collection, such as clipboards, interlocking cubes, stick-on notes, markers, and so on.

For Sessions 2, 3, and 4

- Duplicate Student Sheet 5, Looking at Data, 1 per pair.

For Session 5

- Consider how students will present their data in Session 5. You will need to plan where their data will be displayed and also whom they will make their presentations to. You may want to invite families or other classes for the presentations, or you might choose to have students present to their classmates. See Session 5 for a few ideas about how to organize this presentation.

Choosing a Question to Investigate

Materials

- Chart paper
- Student Sheet 4 (1 per pair)
- Materials for data collection

What Happens

As a class, students brainstorm a list of possible things they could collect data about. In pairs they choose a question to investigate and begin to plan their data analysis project. Their work focuses on:

- considering compelling questions to collect data about
- planning a data analysis project

Start-Up

Today's Number

Calendar Date *and* Number of School Days Suggest that students use multiples of 5 and 10 as you brainstorm ways to express Today's Number. For example, if students are working with the number 29 (calendar date), one possible solution is 25 + 5 − 1. If students are working with a larger number, such as 153, a possible solution is 25 + 25 +20 + 20 + 10 + 35 + 15 + 3. Add a card to the class counting strip and fill in another number on the blank 200 chart if you are keeping track of the number of school days.

Activity

Brainstorming Interesting Questions

During the next five math classes, students will be collecting data about a topic or question that they are interested in. Their work will include deciding on a question to collect data about; planning their project, including how they will collect the data and what materials they will need; organizing and representing the data they collect; and then making some statements about the question they investigated based on the data they collected.

If you are teaching the full-year *Investigations* curriculum and you have completed the unit *Does It Walk, Crawl, or Swim?* your class will have had experience working with categorical data. In this case, you might decide to let students collect either categorical or numerical data. If this unit is your first data unit, it is recommended that you limit students to a project that focuses on numerical data. For the purpose of example, numerical data projects are the focus in this investigation. (You may need to help students make distinctions. They may select an interesting question, not caring if it will generate numerical or categorical data.)

During the last few weeks we collected data about different topics and questions. Early in our work you chose one question from a survey. Last week you collected information about the number of teeth students lost.

In each of those activities you collected data about a question or topic that had already been decided. Now you and a partner will decide on a question that you would like to collect data about. You will collect the data, make a representation of the data, and then make some statements about what your representation tells you.

In order to give students a sense of how this data project will unfold, you may want to write the following schedule on the board:

Monday	Choose a question to investigate Plan the data project
Tuesday	Collect data Organize the data
Wednesday	Make a representation of the data
Thursday	Write about what your data tell you
Friday	Share data projects

Talk with students about any questions they have about the data project. You may want to limit students to collecting data from their classmates. This focuses the project on a specific group and makes the collection of data simpler. Or you may want to let students decide on the population they would like to collect data from. This broadens the potential scope of the project.

Students' comfort level in the school community and how they felt about collecting teeth data from other classes may be helpful information as you make this decision. Students spend no more than half a math session collecting their data. This too may influence your decision.

Brainstorming Interesting Questions Before students begin to plan their data projects, brainstorm questions to investigate. Record their ideas on chart paper and post it in the classroom so they can refer to it. Remind students that their questions need to focus on numerical data and review what types of questions provide numerical responses. The following is a list of questions generated by students:

How many colors are on your socks?

How many people are there in your family?

How many pets do you have?

How many letters are in your first (or last) name?

How many cubes can you hold in one hand?

How many television shows do you watch in one day?

How many buttons are you wearing?

How many times can you write your name in a minute?

How many *S*'s are in your full name?

See the **Teacher Note,** The Teacher's Role in Shaping Questions (p. 80), for more information on helping students generate questions to explore in a data collection project.

❖ **Tip for the Linguistically Diverse Classroom** Draw pictures of rebuses over key words in the questions listed on chart paper as a visual aid for students with limited English proficiency. For example, draw simple sketches of a sock over the word *sock*, stick figures over the word *family*, a dog over the words *pets*, and so on.

Activity

Planning a Data Project

After a list of questions has been generated, organize students into pairs and introduce the data collection project.

Before you begin to collect data, you need to do some planning. First, agree on a question to investigate. You can choose one from our list or think of one on your own. Next, make a plan about how you will collect your data. This includes what materials you will need and how you will keep track of the information that you are collecting.

Distribute Student Sheet 4, Planning a Data Collection Project, to each pair of students. Students will be familiar with this sheet from the previous investigation. Go over the questions on the sheet to make sure students understand the task of planning their project. Let students know that some of them may be interested in collecting data about the same question, but that no more than three pairs of students can work on the same question.

Each pair should answer the questions on the student sheet. When they are finished, they should talk to you about their plan. Before students begin work, remind them that today is a planning day and that during the next session they will begin to collect data.

As students are planning, listen to how they decide on their question, what materials they will need, and how they will collect the data. Offer assistance or suggestions to students who have a difficult time getting organized or whose data project plans exceed the time scope of the project. Support students' plans by asking questions that help them focus on the task and by asking them to talk through their plan.

Resist structuring students' data projects for them. It is more important for them to encounter some of the real problems involved in collecting data based on their own plan rather than to follow a plan that you have outlined, which may not make sense to them. Flaws or problems are likely to be realized by students themselves.

As students finish their plan, have them briefly explain their project to you using Student Sheet 4 as a guide. As each pair of students is ready, they should gather any materials they will need in order to collect their data and store them in a safe place until the following session. Students should also "practice" with their partner how they will ask their question.

You may not have time during class to listen to everyone's data plans, and some students may not finish their plans by the end of this session. Continue the process later in the day or at the beginning of the next session.

Before the Next Session   Think about how you might structure the process of collecting data in your classroom. Students can begin to collect data as soon as they finish their plan. Or students can collect data throughout the school day, not just during math time. This would stagger the number of students asking questions of each other at any one time.

If you need to limit students to collecting data only during math time, and all students are ready to collect data at the same time, organize this so that there isn't a traffic jam of data collectors. For example, you might divide the class into groups and organize the session so that part of the class collects data from the other part, who answers the questions. Then the two groups switch roles.

Students will undoubtedly have a variety of questions that they would like to explore for their data project. Once you have decided whether students will work with categorical data, numerical data, or both, you will need to guide them toward an appropriate question. Students may be interested in questions that are silly or fantastic. Some fantastic questions may be worth pursuing, but you and your students will need to judge whether the question would be embarrassing in any way. If a question seems uninteresting to you or to other students, ask the creator of the question to say something about why he or she is interested and what information he or she hopes to find out.

Sometimes students will ask questions that make them stand out in some way, such as, "How many spider bites have you had?" Or they may ask a question that leads to a different answer for each student (a flat distribution) such as, "How many colors are you wearing?" In these cases, allow students to try out and discover for themselves the issues around such questions. Students may extend their data project by refining their question then collecting data. The question "How many different colors are you wearing on your shirt?" would provide data that is easier to make sense of.

Beware of questions that use numbers as labels, such as, "What's the number on your house?" That question and one such as, "How many people like chocolate ice cream and how many like vanilla ice cream?" seem like numerical data questions but they actually generate categorical data. Additionally, avoid questions that are hard to verify, such as, "How many books have you read?"

Some student-generated ideas for data projects may involve measuring distance or time. "How far can you jump?" or "How big is your foot?" involves students in collecting data by using a linear measurement tool. A question such as "How long can you hold your breath?" or "How long does it take to write your name 10 times?" involves collecting data with a timing device. For their first data project, encourage students to collect data that they can count. Collecting data though measuring time or distance becomes complicated for students to pursue independently, even if you have studied measurement as a class. On the other hand, collecting data through measurement is an excellent example of how data are collected in the real world. If a measuring data project is one that interests students, choose a question to explore together as a class. This way, you can discuss the use of the measuring tools and the class can decide together how best to collect and organize these data. Students will explore collecting data through measurement in grades 3 and 4 of the *Investigations* curriculum.

Finally, keep in mind that students' own data projects may seem less organized than those they have been involved with in Investigations 1 and 2. Students may even appear to have less understanding than you thought. In the past, much of the data analysis process has been structured for students. They have had limited experiences collecting and organizing data and have probably never formulated a data question, which is one of the most difficult steps. Being involved in multiple aspects of the research process is complicated. With their previous data experience and your support in shaping questions, students will be ready to embrace this exciting math project.

Collecting, Organizing, and Representing Data

What Happens

Students collect, organize, and represent the data they have collected. They write a summary describing and interpreting these data. Their work focuses on:

■ collecting, organizing, and representing data
■ interpreting data

Start-Up

Today's Number

Calendar Date *and* Number of School Days Students express Today's Number using pennies, nickels, dimes, and quarters. For example, if Today's Number is 30 (calendar date), a possible combination could be: 25¢ + 5¢ or 10¢ + 10¢ + 5¢ + 5¢. If Today's Number is over 100—for example, 154—one combination could be 25¢ + 25¢ + 25¢ + 25¢ + 25¢ + 25¢ + 1¢ + 1¢ + 1¢ + 1¢. Add a card to the class counting strip and fill in another number on the blank 200 chart if you are keeping track of the number of days in school.

Collecting Pocket Data Sometime during the next three sessions, collect pocket data from students and compare it to the pocket data that you collected in Investigation 1. For more information on this classroom routine, see How Many Pockets? (p. 91).

Materials

■ Student data plans from previous session (completed Student Sheet 4)
■ Materials for data collection
■ Large paper or chart paper (1 per pair)
■ Markers, crayons
■ Student Sheet 5 (1 per pair)

Activity

Collecting the Data

During the first part of this session, students will collect data based on the plans they made during the previous session.

Today, partners will be gathering the data they need for their project. Record all the information you collect and keep track of whom you have collected the information from. When you have finished collecting the data, begin to organize them and then make a representation.

Invite students to share their plans with the class and then begin the data collection process. If some students still need to finish plans or review them with you, get them started. Dismiss the data collectors, then dismiss other students as they finish their plan.

The Data Workshop

Pairs will finish collecting their data at different times. Remind the class that they have three days to collect, organize, and represent their data. Most pairs should finish collecting data by the end of Session 2 and should be organizing and representing their data during Session 3 and the first part of Session 4. During the second part of Session 4, pairs should be working on interpreting their data using Student Sheet 5, and planning how they will present their data during the final session.

These next three math classes can be treated as workshop sessions—a time when pairs are encouraged to work independently on their projects, organize their data, create their representations, and discuss what their representations tell about the question they investigated. During these sessions you can be a resource for students. Some students will function almost independently while others will need more of your support and direction.

If students finish early, encourage them to clarify their representation, to use different materials and represent the same data, or to extend their question by collecting new data about a related question.

During these sessions, spend time observing each pair as they work. Some things you might focus on include:

Keeping track
- How do students record the data they have collected?
- How do they keep track of whom they have collected data from?
- When they are transferring data to their representation, are they able to keep track of each piece of data? Do they include all the data or just some of it?
- Do they check to see that there is one piece of data on their representation for each person they surveyed?

Organizing the data
- When all the data have been collected, how do students organize the information?
- Do they put it in order (from least to most or most to least)?
- Do they group the data?
- Do some students use an interval (0–5, 6–10) to organize the data?

Representing the data
- How do students choose to represent the data?
- Is their representation clear to them? to others?

- Does the representation display an accurate picture of the data collected?
- Have individual students' representations changed during the course of this unit? Do some students use ideas that have been shared previously?

Interpreting Our Data

At the beginning of Session 4, gather students together for a brief discussion about the final phase of their data project.

After you have made your representation of the data, there is one final part of this project that you and your partner need to complete. You should look very carefully at your representation and decide what sorts of information you learned about the question you investigated. The Student Sheet will help you.

Distribute Student Sheet 5, Looking at Data, to each pair of students and review the questions. It may be helpful to refer students to their previous experiences describing and interpreting representations using either the teeth data or the survey data as an example.

❖ **Tip for the Linguistically Diverse Classroom** Suggest that students relate what they did by drawing pictures and writing a few words on Student Sheet 5.

When we were looking at the teeth representations, some people said that as students got older they had lost more teeth. Other people noticed that in first and second grade the data were more spread out on the graph, and in kindergarten and fourth grade they were more clumped together. These are important observations about the data. When you look at your representation, look for special sorts of information that you learned about your question and record those observations on your Student Sheet.

Tomorrow you and your partner will present your projects to the class. When you have finished your observations, you and your partner should rehearse how you will present your project.

Tell students about the presentation process. If you are inviting families or other classes to see the projects, you need to plan with students how and where they will display their data. Each project should include the final representation and Student Sheets 4 and 5. It should also include how students kept track of their data and any preliminary graphs they made.

For the remainder of Session 4, students finish their representations, answer the questions on Student Sheet 5, Looking at Data, and rehearse how they will present their project.

Weekly Log This is a good time for students to record in their Weekly Logs the work that they have done in collecting data. Encourage them to share any problems they are having and any interesting information they have found. They might also enjoy listing all the things they have learned over the past few weeks.

Sessions 2, 3, and 4 Follow-Up

As students finish their data projects, help them display their work around the classroom. You may want to provide each pair with a large sheet of chart or poster paper on which to mount their graphs and their work.

Consider setting up your classroom like a museum, posting data projects along the walls or even in the hallway (if space is limited). When students are presenting their project, they can stand next to their poster while others visit their display.

Data Projects: What Does This Graph Tell Us?

What Happens

Data representations are displayed in the classroom and viewed by students, families, or other invited classes. Students explain their representations to visitors and answer questions about their data project. Their work focuses on:

- using a data representation to communicate information
- interpreting findings based on data

Start-Up

Today's Number

- **Calendar Date**   If you are using the calendar date for Today's Number, work with students to brainstorm ways to express the number using combinations of 10. For example, if the number they are working on is 25 and one number sentence is 10 +10 + 5, ask students if there is another way of making 10, such as (6 + 4) + (6 + 4) + 5 or (4 + 3 + 2 + 1) + (4 + 3 + 2 + 1) + 5. Record their expressions on chart paper.

- **Number of School Days**   If you are using the number of school days for Today's Number, and the number is over 100, encourage students to break apart the number into two parts, such as 100 + 55, and then offer suggestions for how to express one of those numbers, keeping the other intact. For example: 100 + 25 + 25 + 5 or 100 + 10 + 10 +10 + 10 + 10 + 5. Add a card to the class counting strip and fill in another number on the blank 200 chart.

Materials

- Students' data projects displayed around the classroom

Making Data Presentations

The structure of this session will depend on how and to whom students will present their data projects. Whether you are inviting families or other classes of students, or just having students share with classmates, the purpose of this session is the same—to provide students with an opportunity to communicate their findings based on the data they collected and organized.

Inviting Families Some teachers have invited guests to a Data Breakfast at which students, family members, and other guests gather around the data projects and listen to students talk about their project and answer questions. Pairs of students present only once (to their families or invited guests), but there are 15 minutes at the end of the breakfast for guests to circulate around and view other projects.

This is a wonderful opportunity to communicate with families about the mathematical work that is happening in your classroom.

Note: If you invite family members, you may need to arrange for the principal, other adults in the school, or special adults in the students' life to substitute for family members who cannot attend.

Inviting Another Class or Sharing with Classmates If you choose to invite another class to your data presentation or have students share their presentations with their own classmates, the organization can be similar to that of the family presentation. Either assign pairs of visiting students to each pair of presenters or assign pairs of classmates to present to each other.

Assessment
Looking at Representations

As you look at each data project, try to get a sense of how the students collected, organized, represented, and made sense of the data. Data analysis may be a new experience for students, one that they will build on and develop as they have additional opportunities. The goal of assessment is to learn more about where students are as individuals and as a class. As you consider all of the data that students have presented, think about what sorts of interpretations you can begin to make about their experiences with data analysis.

You may not be able to view all the projects during Session 5. Spend time reviewing each project whenever you have a few minutes. Looking at student work can give you some information, but talking with students about their work will give you further insights. As you review students' work and talk to them, consider some of the questions below.

- How do students represent the data they collected? Do you see changes in their representations since the beginning of the unit?

- What process did students use to keep track of their information? Does their graph accurately represent the data collected? Have they left off pieces of information? Is it possible to figure out why information is missing? (Some students might not have an organized way of keeping track; other students might have decided not to include certain information.)

- What sorts of interpretations do students make about their data? Do they describe it? "10 people have 2 pets." Do they make comparisons? "More people own pets than do not own pets." Do they make generalizations or interpretations? "I think more people have pets because we live in the country. I think people who live in the city wouldn't have as many pets."

- Look back through student folders and compare early representations to these data projects.

At some point in the school day, spend a few minutes with students discussing how they felt about their data presentations. What was easy or difficult? How did they feel? Did they learn anything that surprised them?

Choosing Student Work to Save

As the unit ends, you may want to use one of the following options for creating a record of students' work.

- Students look through their folders and think about what they learned in this unit, what they remember most, what was hard or easy for them. You might have students discuss this with partners or share in the whole group.

- Depending on how you organize and collect student work, you may want to have students select some examples of their work to keep in a math portfolio. In addition, you may want to choose some examples from each student's folder to include. Items such as the survey representation, the teeth representation, and the data project can be useful for assessing student growth over the school year.

- Send a selection of work home for families to see. Students can write a cover letter describing their work in this unit. This work should be returned if you are keeping a year-long portfolio of mathematics work for each student.

Today's Number

Today's Number is one of three routines that are built into the grade 2 *Investigations* curriculum. Routines provide students with regular practice in important mathematical ideas such as number combinations, counting and estimating data, and concepts of time. For Today's Number, which is done daily (or most days), students write equations that equal the number of days they have been in school. Each day, the class generates ways to make that number. For example, on the tenth day of school, students look for ways to combine numbers and operations to make 10.

This routine gives students an opportunity to explore some important ideas in number. By generating ways to make the number of the day, they explore:

■ number composition and part-whole relationships (e.g., 10 can be $4 + 6$, $5 + 5$, or $20 - 10$)

■ equivalent arithmetical expressions

■ different operations

■ ways of deriving new numerical expressions by systematically modifying prior ones (e.g., $5 + 5 = 10$, so $5 + 6 = 11$)

Students' strategies evolve over time, becoming more sophisticated as the year progresses. Early in the year, second graders use familiar numbers and combinations, such as $5 + 5 = 10$. As they become accustomed to the routine, they begin to see patterns in the combinations and have favorite kinds of number sentences. Later in the year, they draw on their experiences and increased understanding of number. For example, on the forty-ninth day they might include $100 - 51$, or even $1000 - 951$ in their list of ways to make 49. The types of number sentences that students contribute over time can provide you with a window into their thinking and their levels of understanding of numbers.

If you are doing the full-year grade 2 curriculum, Today's Number is introduced in the first unit, *Mathematical Thinking at Grade 2*. Throughout the curriculum, variations are often introduced as whole-class activities and then carried on in the Start-Up section. The Start-Up section at the beginning of each session offers suggestions of variations and extensions of Today's Number.

While it is important to do Today's Number every day, it is not necessary to do it during math time. In fact, many teachers have successfully included Today's Number as part of their regular routines at the beginning or end of each day. Other teachers incorporate Today's Number into the odd 10 or 15 minutes that exist before lunch or before a transition time.

If you are teaching an *Investigations* unit for the first time, rather than using the number of days you have been in school as Today's Number, you might choose to use the calendar date. (If today is the sixteenth of the month, 16 is Today's Number.) Or you might choose to begin a counting line that does not correspond to the school day number. Each day, add a number to the strip and use this as Today's Number. Begin with the basic activity and then add variations once students become familiar with this routine.

The basic activity is described below, followed by suggested variations.

Materials

■ Chart paper
■ Student Sheet 1, Weekly Log
■ Interlocking cubes

If you are doing the basic activity, you will also need the following materials:

■ Index cards (cut in half and numbered with the days of school so far, e.g., 1 through 5 for the first week of school)

■ Strips of adding-machine tape

■ Blank 200 charts (tape two blank 100 charts together to form a 10-by-20 grid)

Continued on next page

Basic Activity

Initially, you will want to use Today's Number in a whole group, starting the first week of school. After a short time, students will be familiar with the routine and be ready to use it independently.

Establishing the Routine

Step 1. Post the chart paper. Call students' attention to the small box on their Weekly Logs in which they have been recording the number of days they have been in school.

Step 2. Record Today's Number. Write the number of the day at the top of the chart paper. Ask students to suggest ways of making that total.

Step 3. List the number sentences students suggest. Record their suggestions on chart paper. As you do so, invite the group to confirm each suggestion or discuss any incorrect responses, and to explain their thinking. You might have cubes available for students to double-check number sentences.

Step 4. Introduce the class counting strip. Show students the number cards you made and explain that the class is going to create a counting strip. Each day, the number of the day will be added to the row of cards. Post the cards in order in a visible area.

Step 5. Introduce the 200 chart. Display the blank chart and explain that another way the class will keep track of the days in school is by filling in the chart. Record the appropriate numbers in the chart. Tell the class that each day the number of the day will be added to the chart. To help bring attention to landmark numbers on the chart, ask questions such as "How many more days until the tenth day of school? the twentieth day?"

Variations

When students are familiar with the structure of Today's Number, you can connect it to the number work they are doing in particular units.

Make Today's Number Ask students to use some of the following to represent the number:

- only addition
- only subtraction
- both addition and subtraction
- three numbers
- combinations of 10 ($23 = 4 + 6 + 4 + 6 + 3$ or $23 = 1 + 9 + 2 + 8 + 3$)
- a double ($36 = 18 + 18$ or $36 = 4 + 4 + 5 + 5 + 9 + 9$)
- multiples of 5 and 10 ($52 = 10 + 10 + 10 + 10 + 10 + 2$ or $52 = 5 + 15 + 20 + 10 + 2$)
- Use the idea of working backward. Put the number sentences for Today's Number on the board and ask students to determine what number you are expressing: $10 + 3 + 5 + 7 + 5 + 4 = ?$ Notice how students add this string of numbers. Do they use combinations of 10 or doubles to help them?

In addition to defining how Today's Number is expressed, you can vary how and when the activity is done:

Start the Day with Today's Number Post the day's chart paper ahead of time. When students begin arriving, they can generate number sentences and check them with partners, then record their ways to make the number of the day before school begins. Students can review the list of ways to make the number at that time or at the beginning of math class. At whole-group meeting or morning meeting, add the day's number to the 200 chart and the counting strip.

Continued on next page

Choice Time Post chart paper with the Number of the Day written on it so that it is accessible to students. As one of their choices, students generate number sentences and check them with partners, then record them on the chart paper.

Work with a Partner Each student works with a partner for 5 to 10 minutes and lists some ways to make the day's number. Partners check each other's work. Pairs bring their lists to the class meeting or sharing time. Students have their lists of number sentences in their math folders. These can be used as a record of students' growth in working with number over the school year.

Homework Assign Today's Number as homework. Students share number sentences sometime during class the following day.

Catch-Up It can be easy to get a few days behind in this routine, so here are two ways to catch up. Post two or three Number-of-the-Day pages for students to visit during Choice Time or free time. Or assign a Number of the Day to individual students. Each can generate number sentences for his or her number as well as collect number sentences from classmates.

Class History Post "special messages" below the day's number card to create a timeline about your class. Special messages can include birthdays, teeth lost, field trips, memorable events, as well as math riddles.

Today's Number Book Collect the Today's Number charts in a *Number of the Day Book.* Arrange the pages in order, creating chapters based on 10's. Chapter 1, for example, is ways to make the numbers 1 through 10, and combinations for numbers 11–20 become Chapter 2.

How Many Pockets?

How Many Pockets? is one of three classroom routines presented in the grade 2 *Investigations* curriculum. Routines provide students with regular practice in important mathematical ideas such as number combinations, counting and estimating data, and concepts of time. In How Many Pockets? students collect, represent, and interpret numerical data about the number of pockets everyone in the class is wearing on a particular day. This routine often becomes known as Pocket Day. In addition to providing opportunities for comparison of data, Pocket Days provide a meaningful context in which students work purposefully with counting and grouping. Pocket Day experiences contribute to the development of students' number sense—the ability to use numbers flexibly and to see relationships among numbers.

If you are doing the full-year grade 2 *Investigations* curriculum, we suggest that you collect pocket data at regular intervals throughout the year. Many teachers collect pocket data every tenth day of school.

The basic activity is described below, followed by suggested variations. Variations are introduced within the context of the *Investigations* units. If you are not doing the full grade 2 curriculum, we suggest that you begin with the basic activity and then add variations when students become familiar with this routine.

Materials

- Interlocking cubes
- Large jar
- Large rubber band or tape
- Hundred Number Wall Chart and number cards (1–100)
- Pocket Data Chart (teacher made)
- Class list of names
- Chart paper

1	2	3	4	5	6	7	8	9	10
11	12	13	14	15	16	17	18	19	20
21	22	23	24	25	26	27	28	29	30
31	32	33	34	35	36	37	38	39	40
41	42	43	44	45	46	47	48	49	50
51	52	53	54	55	56	57	58	59	60
61	62	63	64	65	66	67	68	69	70
71	72	73	74	75	76	77	78	79	80
81	82	83	84	85	86	87	88	89	90
91	92	93	94	95	96	97	98	99	100

Hundred Number Wall Chart

How many pockets are we wearing today?	Pockets	People
Pocket Day 1		

Pocket Data Chart

Basic Activity

Step 1. Students estimate how many pockets the class is wearing today. Students share their estimates and their reasoning. Record the estimates on chart paper. As the Pocket Days continue through the year, students' estimates may be based on the data recorded on past Pocket Days.

Continued on next page

Step 2. Students count their pockets. Each student takes one interlocking cube for each pocket he or she is wearing.

Step 3. Students put the cubes representing their pockets in a large jar. Vary the way you do this. For example, rather than passing the jar around the group, call on students with specific numbers of pockets to put their cubes in the jar (e.g., students with 3 pockets). Use numeric criteria to determine who puts cubes in the jar (e.g., students with more than 5 but fewer than 8 pockets). Mark the level of cubes on the jar with a rubber band or tape.

Step 4. With students, agree on a way to count the cubes. Count the cubes to find the total number of pockets. Ask students for ideas about how to double-check the count. By re-counting, in another way, students see that a group of objects can be counted in more than one way, for example, by 1's, 2's, 5's, and 10's. With many experiences, they begin to realize that some ways of counting are more efficient than others and that a group of items can be counted in ways other than by 1, without changing the total.

Primary students are usually most secure counting by 1's, and that is often their method of choice. Experiences with counting and grouping in other ways help them begin to see that number is conserved or remains the same regardless of its arrangement—20 cubes is 20 whether counted by 1's, 2's, or 5's. Students also become more flexible in their ability to use grouping, especially important in our number system, in which grouping by 10 is key.

Step 5. Record the total for the day on a Pocket Data Chart. Maintaining a chart of the pocket data as they are accumulated provides natural opportunities for students to see that data can change over time and to compare quantities.

How many pockets are we wearing today?	Pockets	People
Pocket Day 1	41	29

Variations

Comparing Data Students revisit the data from the previous Pocket Day and the corresponding cube level marked on the now empty jar.

On the last Pocket Day, we counted [*give number*] pockets. Do you think we will be wearing more, fewer, or about the same number of pockets today? Why?

After students explain their reasoning, continue with the basic activity. When the cubes have been collected, invite students to compare the present level of cubes with the previous level indicated by the tape or rubber band and to revise their estimates based on this visual information.

Discuss the revised estimates and then complete the activity. After you add the day's total to the Pocket Data Chart, ask students to compare and interpret the data. To facilitate discussion, build a train of interlocking cubes for today's and the previous Pocket Day's number. As students compare the trains, elicit what the cube trains represent and why they have different numbers of cubes.

Use the Hundred Number Wall Chart Do the basic activity, but this time students choose only one way to count the cubes. Then introduce the Hundred Number Wall Chart as a tool that can be used for counting cubes. This is easiest when done with students sitting on the floor in a circle.

Continued on next page

To check our pocket count, we'll put our cubes in the pockets on the chart. A pocket can have just one cube, so we'll put one cube in number 1's pocket, the next cube in number 2's pocket, and keep going in the same way. How many cubes can we put in the first row?

Students will probably see that 10 cubes will fill the first row of the chart.

One group of 10 cubes fits in this row. What if we complete the second row? How many rows of the chart do you think we will fill with the cubes we counted today?

Encourage students to share their thinking. Then have them count with you and help to place the cubes one by one in the pockets on the chart. When finished, examine the chart together, pointing out the total number of cubes in it and the number of complete rows. For each row, snap together the cubes to make a train of 10. As you do so, use the rows to encourage students to consider combining groups of 10. Record the day's total on your Pocket Data Chart.

Note: If cubes do not fit in the pockets of the chart, place the chart on the floor and place the cubes on top of the numbers.

Find the Most Common Number of Pockets
Each student connects the cubes representing his or her pockets into a train. Before finding the total number of pockets, sort the cube trains with students to find the most common number of pockets. Pose and investigate additional questions, such as:

■ How many people are wearing the greatest number of pockets?

■ Is there a number of pockets no one is wearing?

■ Who has the fewest pockets?

The cubes are then counted to determine the total number of pockets.

Take a Closer Look at Pocket Data Each student builds a cube train representing his or her pockets. Beginning with those who have zero

pockets, call on students to bring their cube trains to the front of the room. Record the information in a chart, such as the one shown here. You might make a permanent chart with blanks for placing number cards.

_0_ people have 0 pockets.   _0 pockets_

_4_ people have 1 pocket.   _4 pockets_

_2_ people have 2 pockets.   _4 pockets_

_2_ people have 3 pockets.   _6 pockets_

Pose questions about the data, such as "Two people have 2 pockets. How many pockets is that?" Then record the number of pockets.

To work with combining groups, you might keep a running total of pockets as data are recorded in the chart until you have found the cumulative total.

We counted [12] pockets, and then we counted [6] pockets. How many pockets have we counted so far? Be ready to tell us how you thought about it.

As students give their solutions, encourage them to share their mental strategies. Alternatively, after all data have been collected, students can work on the problem of finding the total number of pockets.

Graphing Pocket Data Complete the activity using the variation Find the Most Common Number of Pockets. Leave students' cube trains intact. Each student then creates a representation of the day's pocket data. Provide a variety of materials including stick-on notes, stickers or paper squares, markers and crayons, drawing paper, and graph paper, for students to use.

Continued on next page

These cube trains represent how many pockets people are wearing today. Suppose you want to show our pocket data to your family, friends, or students in another classroom. How could you show our pocket data on paper so that someone else could see what we found out about our pockets today?

By creating their own representations, students become more familiar with the data and may begin to develop theories as they consider how to communicate what they know about the data to an audience. Students' representations may not be precise; what's important is that the representations enable them to describe and interpret their data.

Compare Pocket Data with Another Class
Arrange ahead of time to compare pocket data with a fourth- or fifth-grade class. Present the following question to students:

Do you think fifth-grade students wear more, fewer, or about the same number of pockets as second-grade students? Why?

Discuss students' thinking. Then investigate this question by comparing your data with data from another classroom. One way to do this is to invite the other class to participate in your Pocket Day. Do the activity first with the second graders, recording on the Pocket Data Chart how many people have each number of pockets and finding the total number of pockets. Repeat with the other students, recording their data on chart paper. Then compare the two sets of data.

How does the number of pockets in the fifth grade compare to the number of pockets in second grade?

Discuss students' ideas.

Calculate the Total Number of Pockets Divide students into groups of four or five. Each group determines the total number of pockets being worn by the group. Data from each small group are shared and recorded on the board. Using this information, students work in pairs to determine the total number of pockets worn by the class. As a group, they share strategies used for determining the total number of pockets.

In another variation, students share individual pocket data with the group. Each student records this information using a class list of names to keep track. They then determine the total number of pockets worn by the students in the class. Observe how students calculate the total number of pockets. What materials do they use? Do they group familiar numbers together, such as combinations of 10, doubles, or multiples of 5?

Time and Time Again

Time and Time Again is one of three classroom routines included in the grade 2 *Investigations* curriculum. This routine helps students develop an understanding of time-related ideas such as sequencing of events, the passage of time, duration of time periods, and identifying important times in their day.

Because many of the ideas and suggestions presented in this routine will be incorporated throughout the school day and into other parts of the curriculum, we encourage teachers to use this routine in whatever way meets the needs of their students and their classroom. We believe that learning about time and understanding ideas about time happen best when activities are presented *over* time and have relevance to students' experiences and lives.

Daily Schedule Post a daily schedule. Identify important times (start of school, math, music, recess, reading) using both analog (clockface) and digital (10:15) representations. Discuss the daily schedule each day and encourage students to compare the actual starting time of, say, math class with what is posted on the schedule.

Talk Time Identify times as you talk with students. For example, "In 15 minutes we will be cleaning up and going to recess." Include specific times and refer to a clock in your classroom: "It is now 10:15. In 15 minutes we will be cleaning up and going out to recess. That will be at 10:30."

Timing One Hour Set a timer to go off at 1-hour intervals. Choose a starting time and write both the analog time (use a clockface) and the digital time. When the timer rings, record the time using analog and digital times. At the end of the day, students make observations about the data collected. Initially you'll want to use whole and half hours as your starting points. Gradually you can use times that are 10 or 20 minutes after the hour and also appoint students to be in charge of the timer and of recording the times.

Timing Other Intervals Set a timer to go off at 15-minute intervals over a period of 2 hours. Begin at the hour and after the data have been collected, discuss with students what happened each time 15 minutes was added to the time (11:00, 11:15, 11:30, 11:45). You can also try this with 10-minute intervals.

Home Schedule Students make a schedule of important times at home. They can do this both for school days and for nonschool days. They should include both analog and digital times on their schedules. Later in the year they can use this schedule to see if they were really on time for things like dinner, piano lessons, or bedtime. They record the actual time that events happened and calculate how early or late they were. Students can illustrate their schedules.

Comparing Schedules Partners compare important times in their day, such as what time they eat dinner, go to bed, get up, leave for school. They can compare whether events are earlier or later, and some students might want to calculate how much earlier or later these events occur.

Life Line Students create a timeline of their life. They interview family members and collect information about important developmental milestones such as learning to walk, first word, first day of school, first lost tooth, and important family events. Students then record these events on a life line that is a representation of the first seven or eight years of their lives.

Clock Data Students collect data about the types of clocks they have in their home—digital or analog. They make a representation of these data and as a class compare their results.

- **Are there more digital or analog clocks in your house?**
- **Is this true of our class set of data?**
- **How could we compare our individual data to a class set of data?**

Continued on next page

Time Collection Students bring in things from home that have to do with time. Include digital and analog clocks as well as timers of various sorts. These items could be sorted and grouped in different ways. Some students may be interested in investigating different types of timepieces such as sundials, sand timers, and pendulums.

How Long Is a Minute? As you time 1 minute, students close their eyes and then raise their hands when they think a minute has gone by. Ask, "Is a minute longer or shorter than you imagined?" Repeat this activity or have students do this with partners. You can also do this activity with a half-minute.

What Can You Do in a Minute? When students are familiar with timing 1 minute, they work in pairs and collect data about things they can do in 1 minute. Brainstorm a list of events that students might try. Some ideas that second graders have suggested include writing their names; doing jumping jacks or sit-ups; hopping on one foot; saying the ABC's; snapping together interlocking cubes; writing certain numbers or letters (this is great practice for working on reversals); and drawing geometric shapes such as triangles, squares, or stars. Each student chooses four or five activities to do in 1 minute. Before they collect the data, they predict how many they can do in 1 minute. Then with partners they gather the data and compare.

How Long Does It Take? Using a stopwatch or a clock with a second hand, time how long it takes students to complete certain tasks such as lining up, giving out supplies, or cleaning up after math time. Emphasize doing these things in a responsible way. Students can take turns being "timekeepers."

Stopwatches Most second graders are fascinated by stopwatches. You will find that students come up with many ideas about what to time. If possible, acquire a stopwatch for your classroom. (Inexpensive ones are available through educational supply catalogs.) Having stopwatches available in the classroom allows students to teach each other about time and how to keep track of time.

The following activities will help ensure that this unit is comprehensible to students who are acquiring English as a second language. The suggested approach is based on *The Natural Approach: Language Acquisition in the Classroom* by Stephen D. Krashen and Tracy D. Terrell (Alemany Press, 1983.)The intent is for second language learners to acquire new vocabulary in an active, meaningful context.

Note that *acquiring* a word is different from *learning* a word. Depending on their level of proficiency, students may be able to comprehend a word upon hearing it during an investigation, without being able to say it. Other students may be able to use the word orally, but not read or write it. The goal is to help students naturally acquire targeted vocabulary at their present level of proficiency.

We suggest using these activities just before the related investigations. The activities can be led by English-proficient students.

Investigation 1

age, how old, younger, older

1. If possible, display photos or pictures cut from magazines of a baby, an elementary school child, a teenager, a middle-age adult, and a grandparent. (Or you may want to draw representations on the chalkboard.) Talk about how old each person pictured might be. Ask students to guess their ages. Continue discussion until students have reached a consensus of the estimated age for each person.

2. As you point to each picture, ask students to decide whether they are older or youger than the person pictured.

siblings, brothers, sisters

1. Show students a photo or a magazine picture of a family. (The family should have two or more children.) Identify its members as you point to each person. Help students to make the distinction that a family may have three chidren, but each child has two siblings. Ask students questions about the picture. **How many children are in this family?** Point to the individual children.

How many brothers and sisters does this child have?

How about this child? How many brothers and sisters does he (she) have?

Investigation 2

organize, order

1. Gather a group of objects, such as buttons, that can be organized by a visual attribute. Show students one way to organize the objects, such as by color.

   Is there another way we could organize these buttons? (size, shape)

   Have students group the buttons by their suggested criteria.

2. Begin ordering the buttons in some way, such as from smallest to largest. After putting a few in this order, challenge students to decide which button would be next in line, until all buttons are placed.

3. Ask sudents to shut their eyes, and move two or three buttons so they are no longer in size order. Then ask students to look at the sequence of buttons again.

   Are the buttons still in the size order? Do you see any that are out of size order?

lost, missing

1. Write numbers such as these on the board.
   4   6   2   9   12   7   10

   Ask students to order the numbers from smallest to largest. Write the new order on the chalkboard.

2. Ask questions about numbers missing from the sequence.

   Is there a number missing between 4 and 6? What number is it?

   Emphasize that the number is not lost, it is just not included in this sequence.

Blackline Masters

Family Letter
Student Sheet 1, Weekly Log
Student Sheet 2, Surveys
Student Sheet 3, Teeth Data
Student Sheet 4, Planning a Data Collection Project
Student Sheet 5, Looking at Data
Student Sheet 6, Mystery Teeth Data, Class A
Student Sheet 7, Mystery Teeth Data, Class B
Student Sheet 8, Mystery Teeth Data, Class C
Student Sheet 9, Mystery Teeth Data, Class D
Student Sheet 10, Which Class Is It? (Classes A–D)
Student Sheet 11, Which Class Is It? (Recording Sheet)

_____, 19____

Dear Family,

For the next few weeks our class will be working on a mathematics unit called *How Many Pockets? How Many Teeth?* This unit introduces children to collecting, organizing, and representing numerical information about a group of people. Children will collect and represent data about how many pockets they have on, how many siblings they have, how old they are, and how many letters are in their name. Throughout the unit, children will be introduced to a variety of ways of representing the data they collect. They will also be encouraged to develop their own representations of data.

Since losing teeth is such an important subject for second graders, the focus of one investigation is to collect data about the number of teeth lost. Children will use this information as well as data collected from their older and younger siblings to predict how many teeth they expect children in older and younger grades to have lost. They will investigate this question further by collecting teeth data from other classrooms in the school and comparing the real data with their hypotheses.

In the final project of the unit, students will design their own data collection project based on a question they are interested in investigating.

While our class is working on this unit, you can help in these ways:

- For homework your child will be collecting information about how many teeth older or younger siblings have lost. (Children with no siblings can ask a friend.) As your child collects and records this information, you can ask him or her to predict how many teeth an older (or younger) sibling has, or you might even let him or her count the number of teeth you have! Some children may be interested in a further investigation about the number of teeth different animals have. Your library can be a resource for this information.

- As you are reading the newspaper or a magazine, point out various graphs and charts to your child and talk about how you make sense of them, what they mean, and why you're interested in them. This is an opportunity for you to show your child how graphs communicate important information to you and your family.

Thank you for your help making math interesting and fun for your child.

Sincerely,

Weekly Log

Day Box

Monday, _____

Tuesday, _____

Wednesday, _____

Thursday, _____

Friday, _____

Surveys

1. How many pets do you have? _____

2. How many shoelace holes do you have on today? _____

    _____

3. How many pieces of pizza do you usually eat for dinner?

    _____

4. How many letters are in your first name? _____

- -

Name _____   Date _____

Student Sheet 2

Surveys

1. How many pets do you have? _____

2. How many shoelace holes do you have on today? _____

    _____

3. How many pieces of pizza do you usually eat for dinner?

    _____

4. How many letters are in your first name? _____

Teeth Data

1. How many people did you collect data from? How did you

   check? _____

2. Describe the shape of your representation. _____

   _____

3. What's the fewest number of teeth lost in our class? _____

   How many people lost that many teeth? _____

4. What's the greatest number of teeth lost in our class? _____

   How many people lost that many teeth? _____

5. Is there any number of teeth that no one has lost? _____

   Which one(s)? _____

6. How many people lost between 0 and 4 teeth? _____

   How many people lost between 5 and 8 teeth? _____

7. Which group lost more, 0–4 or 5–8? _____

8. Is there anything that you think is unusual about the teeth data we

   collected? _____

   _____

Planning a Data Collection Project

1. What are you collecting data about? _____

   _____

2. Whom will you collect data from? _____

3. What question will you ask? _____

   _____

4. How will you collect these data? What's your plan? _____

   _____

   _____

   _____

5. What materials will you need? _____

   _____

   _____

   _____

   _____

Looking at Data

1. Whom did you collect data from? _____

2. What was your data question? _____

3. How many people did you collect data from? _____

4. How many pieces of data do you have on your

   representation? _____

5. Describe the shape of your representation. _____

   _____

6. What are two interesting things about the data you collected?

   _____

   _____

7. Is there anything about the data you collected that surprised you?

   _____

8. What did you learn about the question you collected data

   about? (Use the back of this sheet if you need more space.)

   _____

Mystery Teeth Data, Class A

Alyssa	14 teeth
Brian	11 teeth
Danny	8 teeth
Daniel	6 teeth
Evan	8 teeth
Ellie	8 teeth
Erica	9 teeth
Gordon	8 teeth
Howard	11 teeth
Karen	13 teeth
Jan	13 teeth
Jacob	12 teeth
Lily	7 teeth
Maeve	6 teeth
Mary	7 teeth
Maude	8 teeth
Nadeem	5 teeth
Nadir	7 teeth
Noah	8 teeth
Rachel	8 teeth
Ricardo	8 teeth
Sarah	8 teeth
Sammy	7 teeth
Steve	6 teeth
Tracey	9 teeth
Yanni	8 teeth

Mystery Teeth Data, Class B

Angel	7 teeth
Ayaz	6 teeth
Bjorn	1 tooth
Camilla	7 teeth
Chen	3 teeth
Crystal	13 teeth
Ebony	8 teeth
Franco	6 teeth
Graham	8 teeth
Harris	9 teeth
Helena	8 teeth
Imani	8 teeth
Jeffrey	9 teeth
Jess	3 teeth
Karina	9 teeth
Laura	12 teeth
Lila	8 teeth
Linda	8 teeth
Lionel	5 teeth
Naomi	8 teeth
Paul	8 teeth
Ping	4 teeth
Samir	9 teeth
Simon	6 teeth
Tim	8 teeth
Tory	8 teeth

Mystery Teeth Data, Class C

Alfonso	2 teeth
Alexandra	2 teeth
Andrew	1 tooth
Anthony	0 teeth
Brandon	1 tooth
Britney	1 tooth
Carle	4 teeth
Clarence	0 teeth
Daniel	1 tooth
Eric	0 teeth
Esther	0 teeth
Gordon	3 teeth
Grace	0 teeth
Isaac	2 teeth
Jackie	0 teeth
Jeremiah	3 teeth
Jonathan	0 teeth
Jordan	2 teeth
Katherine	3 teeth
Latoya	1 tooth
Megan	0 teeth
Myles	1 tooth
Ned	3 teeth
Paul	0 teeth
Percy	0 teeth
Yoshi	0 teeth

Mystery Teeth Data, Class D

Aaron	10 teeth
Allana	11 teeth
Ben	5 teeth
Botan	8 teeth
Carla	9 teeth
Chi Wan	12 teeth
Dyala	14 teeth
Jesse	9 teeth
Julie	14 teeth
Kevin	9 teeth
Kira	10 teeth
Laura	7 teeth
Liana	8 teeth
Lois	11 teeth
Lori	12 teeth
Morgan	13 teeth
Nat	8 teeth
Ramon	14 teeth
Roshma	13 teeth

Which Class Is It? (Classes A-D)

Class A		Class B		Class C		Class D	
Alyssa	14 teeth	Angel	7 teeth	Alfonso	2 teeth	Aaron	10 teeth
Brian	11 teeth	Ayaz	6 teeth	Alexandra	2 teeth	Allana	11 teeth
Danny	8 teeth	Bjorn	1 tooth	Andrew	1 tooth	Ben	5 teeth
Daniel	6 teeth	Camilla	7 teeth	Anthony	0 teeth	Botan	8 teeth
Evan	8 teeth	Chen	3 teeth	Brandon	1 tooth	Carla	9 teeth
Ellie	8 teeth	Crystal	13 teeth	Britney	1 tooth	Chi Wan	12 teeth
Erica	9 teeth	Ebony	8 teeth	Carle	4 teeth	Dyala	14 teeth
Gordon	8 teeth	Franco	6 teeth	Clarence	0 teeth	Jesse	9 teeth
Howard	11 teeth	Graham	8 teeth	Daniel	1 tooth	Julie	14 teeth
Karen	13 teeth	Harris	9 teeth	Eric	0 teeth	Kevin	9 teeth
Jan	13 teeth	Helena	8 teeth	Esther	0 teeth	Kira	10 teeth
Jacob	12 teeth	Imani	8 teeth	Gordon	3 teeth	Laura	7 teeth
Lily	7 teeth	Jeffrey	9 teeth	Grace	0 teeth	Liana	8 teeth
Maeve	6 teeth	Jess	3 teeth	Isaac	2 teeth	Lois	11 teeth
Mary	7 teeth	Karina	9 teeth	Jackie	0 teeth	Lori	12 teeth
Maude	8 teeth	Laura	12 teeth	Jeremiah	3 teeth	Morgan	13 teeth
Nadeem	5 teeth	Lila	8 teeth	Jonathan	0 teeth	Nat	8 teeth
Nadir	7 teeth	Linda	8 teeth	Jordan	2 teeth	Ramon	14 teeth
Noah	8 teeth	Lionel	5 teeth	Katherine	3 teeth	Roshma	13 teeth
Rachel	8 teeth	Naomi	8 teeth	Latoya	1 tooth		
Ricardo	8 teeth	Paul	8 teeth	Megan	0 teeth		
Sarah	8 teeth	Ping	4 teeth	Myles	1 tooth		
Sammy	7 teeth	Samir	9 teeth	Ned	3 teeth		
Steve	6 teeth	Simon	6 teeth	Paul	0 teeth		
Tracey	9 teeth	Tim	8 teeth	Percy	0 teeth		
Yanni	8 teeth	Tory	8 teeth	Yoshi	0 teeth		

Which Class Is It? (Recording Sheet)

1. How did you decide which set of Mystery Data went with your representation?

2. What grade level do you think it represents and why?